Y0-BRX-379

795

KINGS &
QUEENS

Vicky Wood

This first edition published in Great Britain in 2012 by
Crimson Publishing Ltd
Westminster House
Kew Road
Richmond
Surrey
TW9 2ND

© Crimson Publishing Ltd, 2012

The right of Vicky Wood to be identified as the author of this work has been asserted by her in accordance with the Copyright, Designs and Patents Act, 1988.

All rights reserved. No part of this publication may be reproduced, transmitted in any form or by any means, or stored in a retrieval system without either the prior written permission of the publisher, or in the case of reprographic reproduction a licence issued in accordance with the terms and licences issued by the CLA Ltd.

A catalogue record for this book is available from the British Library.

ISBN 978 1 78059 075 2

Designed and typeset by Michael King

Printed and bound by Craft Print, Singapore

CONTENTS

INTRODUCTION

From the earliest monarchs taking command of Britain by force to the modern-day royal family, the history of the monarchy has been a dangerous, exciting and dramatic one, with war, murder, tradition and ceremony reigning side by side.

EARLY ENGLISH RULERS V. THE VIKINGS

England was invaded by the Romans in AD43 and became a part of the Roman Empire for almost 400 years (see p.14) until they abandoned their claim. Afterwards, the country was divided into seven different kingdoms, each one ruled by its own monarch (see p.17).

Throughout this period, the country was subject to a series of Viking invasions from Scandinavia. It was through these battles that Alfred the Great of the kingdom of Wessex emerged as the undefeated ruler and his grandson Athelstan became the first ruler of a united England. The Vikings hadn't given up, though and in 1016, the Danish King Canute succeeded in winning the English crown for 19 years (see p.17).

Coronation of Queen Victoria in 1837

UNITED KINGDOM

Until the 12th century England, Ireland and Scotland were separate kingdoms with Wales a principality. Then in the late 12th century the kings of England claimed the lordship of Ireland taking advantage of infighting amongst the Irish rulers.

This was the beginning of almost 700 years of direct rule by England, until 1922 when Ireland was partitioned with only the six northern countries, part of the Ulster province, remaining under the control of Westminster in England.

 DID YOU KNOW?
The Imperial State Crown, worn by the Queen for state occasions, is transported in a bullet-proof coach, as it is considered to be irreplaceable.

In 1282 Edward I invaded Wales, and took control of the region when the Prince of Wales, Llywelyn ap Gruffydd, was killed in battle. Wales came under England's control and 'Prince of Wales' is still the title of the monarch's eldest son (see p.36)

Scotland and England united under the same crown in 1603, when James VI of Scotland, next in line to the English throne, succeeded after the death of the childless Elizabeth I (see p.66).

One of the Household Cavalry

'Uneasy lies the head that wears a crown.'
William Shakespeare, Henry IV Part I

The United Kingdom was officially created following the Acts of Union in 1801.

FOREIGN INVASIONS

King Canute's invasion in 1016 wasn't the only successful invasion of Britain. When William of Normandy won the Battle of Hastings in 1066, he took the crown for himself.

During constant wars with France throughout the 14th century (see p.40), with the Spanish Armada in the 16th century (see p.63) and the two World Wars in the 20th century (see pp.88–91) Britain's kings and queens have had to defend and lead their country.

PAGEANTRY OF MONARCHY

The greatest strength of the monarchy lies in their ability to change with the times. Beginning with the absolute power of medieval rulers, the monarchy has now become a constitutional one, ruling closely with Parliament and the prime minister. The role of the monarch is now more ceremonial and traditional but still a vital part of British heritage.

 IF YOU LIKED THIS...
Visit Westminster Abbey, Buckingham Palace (open to the public in August and September) or Windsor Castle.

TOP 10 TURNING POINTS

On this page are 10 pivotal moments associated with the British monarchy, ranging from wars, murders and executions to the power of the British Empire. These moments were turning points in British history, so read on to find out more.

1 BATTLE OF HASTINGS

William, Duke of Normandy, determined to claim the throne of England, killed Harold II at the Battle of Hastings in 1066 and ruled England successfully for over 20 years. For more details, see p.20.

2 MAGNA CARTA

King John was such an unpopular ruler, that the English noblemen forced him to sign the Magna Carta in 1215, limiting the monarch's powers (see p.34).

3 EDWARD I'S WAR WITH SCOTLAND

Edward I's wars against Scotland made the names of William Wallace, and Robert the Bruce (who later became King of Scotland) legendary. For more details, see p.38.

ROBERT
THE
BRUCE
KING
OF
SCOTS
1306-1329

4 100 YEARS WAR

To strengthen their claim to the French throne, the English monarchs declared war on France. Among the most notable people of this time were Henry V and Joan of Arc, the peasant girl who led an army to victory (see p.18).

5 WARS OF THE ROSES

In the 15th century, two branches of the royal family fought for the throne. These wars led to the murder of at least one king in the Tower of London (see p.50) and another being killed in battle (see p.51).

6 CIVIL WAR AND EXECUTION OF A KING

In the 1640s, civil war broke out between Charles I and Parliament. Charles I lost and was executed. Under Oliver Cromwell Parliament ran the country for 11 years before the monarchy was restored (see p.68).

7 HENRY VIII'S SIX WIVES

Henry VIII is infamous for having six wives and even more infamous for having two of them executed in the Tower of London. To discover more about the fate of his six wives, see p.58.

8 PRINCES IN THE TOWER

The disappearance of 12-year-old Edward V and his younger brother from the Tower of London is a mystery to this day (see p.50).

9 THE REGENCY

When George III, believed to be mad, could no longer rule the country, his son took over as Prince Regent. During this period, the royal family became highly unpopular, due to their extravagance and scandalous private lives (see p.79).

10 THE BRITISH EMPIRE

By 1900, Britain had an empire which stretched from one end of the globe to the other, taking in over a fifth of the world's population. For more information see p.84.

TIMELINE

**AD43
Roman invasion
p.14**

**1085
Domesday
Book
p.24**

**1066
Battle of
Hastings
p.20**

**1100
William II
is killed
p.25**

AD43   1066

✚ **Ancient Kings and the Saxons**   ✠ **The Normans**

(pp.14–21)
Tribal kings: prior to AD43
Romans: AD43–AD400
Saxons: AD400–1066
Alfred the Great: AD871–AD899
Edward the Confessor: 1042–66
Harold II: 1066

(pp.22–27)
William I: 1066–87
William II: 1087–1100
Henry I: 1100–35
Stephen: 1135–54

**William the
Conqueror
1066–87
p.24**

**Alfred
the Great
AD871–AD899
p.17**

**1290s
Scottish Wars
p.38**

**1483
Princes in the Tower
p.50**

**1170
Thomas
Beckett
murdered
p.30**

**1455–85
The Wars
of the
Roses
p.44**

1154

1399

1485

 The Plantagenets

 The Houses of Lancaster and York

(pp.28–41)
Henry II: 1154–89
Richard I: 1189–99
John: 1199–1216
Henry III: 1216–72
Edward I: 1272–1307
Edward II: 1307–27
Edward III: 1327–77
Richard II: 1377–99

(pp.42–51)
Henry IV: 1399–1413
Henry V: 1413–22
Henry VI: 1422–61; 1470–71
Edward IV: 1461–70; 1471–83
Edward V: 1483
Richard III: 1483–85

**Richard I
1189–99
p.31**

**Henry V
1413–22
p.47**

**1531
Creation
of the
Church of
England
p.56**

**1605 Gunpowder Plot
p.66**

**1587
Execution
of Mary,
Queen of
Scots
p.63**

**1629–40
The Civil War
p.68**

1485

1603

 The Tudors

The Stuarts

(pp.52–63)
Henry VII: 1485–1509
Henry VIII: 1509–47
Edward VI: 1547–53
Mary I: 1553–58
Elizabeth I: 1558–1603

(pp.64–73)
James I: 1603–25
Charles I: 1625–49
Charles II: 1660–85
James II: 1685–88
William III and Mary II: 1689–1702
Anne: 1702–14

**Elizabeth I
1558–1603
p.62**

**Charles I
1625–49
p.67**

**1746
Battle of Culloden
p.79**

**2012
Elizabeth II's
Diamond Jubilee
p.93**

**1939–45
Second
World War
p.88**

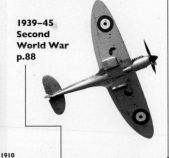

**1775–83
American
War of
Independence
p.74**

1714   1910   present

 The House of Hanover   **The Windsors**

(pp.74–85)
George I: 1714–27
George II: 1727–60
George III: 1760–1820
Regency: 1811–20
George VI: 1820–30
William IV: 1830–37
Victoria: 1837–1901
Edward VII: 1901–10

(pp.86–93)
George V: 1910–36
Edward VIII: 1936
George VI: 1936–52
Elizabeth II: 1952–

**George VI
1936–52
p.90**

**Victoria
1837–1901
p.82**

WELSH, SCOTTISH AND IRISH KINGS

Kings of Scotland were crowned at the stone of Scone

EARLY HISTORY OF THE SCOTTISH KINGS

Until the ninth century AD, Scotland was divided up into several kingdoms, including the Highlands where the Picts ruled and Dalriata (present-day Argyllshire). These two kingdoms were united under Kenneth MacAlpin in the AD840s; he is now regarded as being the first King of a united Scotland. Amongst the most famous of these early kings was Macbeth, immortalised in the play by William Shakespeare.

HOUSES OF CANMORE AND STEWART

The House of Canmore began with Malcolm III in 1058. He was named *Ceann Mor* which meant 'Great Chief'. The death of Queen Margaret in 1290, last in the direct line, brought about war with Edward I of England (see p.36) and ended with Robert the Bruce's success in being recognised as independent King of Scotland in 1328 (see p.39).

DID YOU KNOW?
Malcolm III's daughter, Matilda (Edith), married Henry I of England (see p.26).

Robert the Bruce's daughter married into the Stewart family, making them the ruling family. One of the most famous rulers of the House of Stewart was Mary, Queen of Scots. It was her son, James VI, who united the crowns and became King of England in 1603, after the death of the last Tudor English monarch, Elizabeth I (see p.66).

IF YOU LIKED THIS...
Visit Edinburgh Castle to see the Stone of Scone; the Stone was where the Kings of Scotland were crowned until Edward I took it to England. It was returned to Scotland in 1996.

EARLY RULERS OF WALES
As with Scotland, Wales was divided into tribal areas ruled by chieftains. In the mid-ninth century, Rhodri Mawr ('the Great') united Wales, but on his death he left the kingdom to his sons, causing Wales to divide again.

By the 1000s, Wales was divided into four principalities: Gwynedd, Powys, Deheubarth and Glamorgan. War with England was almost constant after William I of England (see p.24) installed noblemen on the borders of Wales, who regularly attacked the country.

These border lords had conquered most of Wales by the 1100s. This changed under the rule of Lord Rhys, ruler of Deheubarth, who regained almost all of the lost territory. Henry II, realising that it was better to have him as an ally, recognised him as the most powerful Welsh ruler, in return for Rhys swearing homage to him.

By the 1240s, Llywelyn the Great, ruler of Gwynedd, had united most of Wales and is regarded as being the first Prince of Wales. His grandson Llywelyn ap Gruffydd, was killed in battle against Edward I of England, who then took over Wales and named his eldest son, Edward, as Prince of Wales, marking the end of independent rule in Wales (see p.36).

EARLY HISTORY OF THE IRISH KINGS

Ireland was divided into a series of provinces, ruled over by their own monarchs. The Ui Neill clan of Ulster were the most powerful, controlling the northern part of Ireland, but their rule came to an end in the 10th century, when Brian Boru, King of Munster, fighting successfully against the invading Vikings, declared himself High King of Ireland. For over 100 years after his death, the kingdom was fought over by rival rulers.

IRELAND V. ENGLAND

The last King of Ireland was Rhuaidri. However, when the deposed King of Leinster sought English help in regaining his kingdom, this gave Henry II an excuse to invade Ireland. Rhuaidri's power was reduced and he gave up the throne at the end of the 12th century. The English monarchy immediately claimed the lordship of Ireland.

In 1542, an Act of Parliament replaced the 'Lordship of Ireland' with the 'Kingdom of Ireland', making the Kings and Queens of England monarchs of Ireland.

 IF YOU LIKED THIS...
Visit the Hill of Tara in County Meath, Ireland. It is believed to be the site where the High Kings of Ireland were inaugurated until the Norman invasion in the 12th century.

This stone marks the spot where Ireland's legendary kings were crowned

Ancient Kings and The Saxons

When the Romans invaded England in AD43, this caused trouble with the tribal rulers who controlled the country at the time and several rebellions took place before the Romans were accepted as rulers.

TRIBAL KINGS BEFORE THE ROMANS

Little is known of the tribal rulers who were here before the Romans invaded. The main historical sources come from the Romans. According to the Roman historian, Tacitus, there were approximately 30 tribes covering the area of present-day England, Scotland and Wales, each with their own ruler.

 IF YOU LIKED THIS...
Visit the Lindow Man in the British Museum. Druid priests of the Celtic tribes may have sacrificed members of the tribes to the Gods; this is possibly so in the case of the Lindow Man.

ROMAN INVASION

In AD41, Claudius became Roman Emperor. Regarded as being weak, he knew he had to strengthen his position with a military victory and set his sights on Britain. The Romans seized control of the south and set up Colchester as their capital. By AD57, most of Britain was under Roman control.

REBEL OR CONFORM?

Most of the local tribes submitted to Roman rule but the Catuvellauni tribe in eastern England, one of the largest and most powerful tribes in the country, did not. Its ruler, Caractacus, hated the Romans and made a determined attempt to drive them out of England. He was defeated and fled.

BOUDICCA, QUEEN OF THE ICENI

The most famous challenge to the Romans' early rule in Britain was the rebellion led by Queen Boudicca of the Iceni tribe in East Anglia in AD60–1.

Boudicca's husband, Prastagus, had supported the Romans, but on his death, the Romans decided to rule the Iceni themselves, even flogging Boudicca and raping her daughters to make them submit to Roman rule. This was a huge mistake. Boudicca rose up against the Romans and burned down their chief cities of Colchester, St Albans and London. Her army was eventually defeated by the Roman governor, Suetonius Paullinus. Boudicca is said to have committed suicide, but no-one knows where she is buried.

WEIRD AND WONDERFUL

There is a story that Boudicca is buried underneath platform 10 at King's Cross station.

ROMAN BRITAIN

After Boudicca's revolt, there were no more serious rebellions led against the Romans. The Romans concentrated on building up Britain and Roman remains can still be seen all over the country. One example is Hadrian's Wall which was built in the north of England to mark the limits of Roman territory as the Romans found it impossible to defeat the tribes in Scotland.

Britain was under Roman control for almost 400 years, before the Romans left in AD410.

IF YOU LIKED THIS...

Visit Hadrian's Wall in the north of England, Tower Hill station in London (where there is still a section of the Roman wall) and the Guildhall Art Gallery in the City of London, where there are remains of the Roman amphitheatre. You can also visit the Museum of London, which gives the whole history of London, starting from the Roman period.

Statue of Queen Boudicca

15

DARK AGES

AD400 TO AD1000

Perceptions of this period as being a backward one have been challenged by recent archaeological discoveries. One of the most famous personalities of this time was King Arthur.

THE 'DARK AGES': TRUE OR FALSE?

There are two possible reasons as to why this period is called the Dark Ages. One is that intellectualism and links abroad reached their lowest point; another is because very little is known about it. However, the discovery of the ship burial at Sutton Hoo in East Anglia in the 1930s, containing jewels and objects from abroad, changed the view of this time, showing that there was both wealth and trading during the Dark Ages.

IF YOU LIKED THIS...
Visit the Sutton Hoo treasure (including the helmet pictured above) at the British Museum.

KING ARTHUR

Although King Arthur is one of the most famous figures of this period, he is probably fictional. He is mentioned in the ninth-century *Historia Brittonum* as a general fighting against the Anglo-Saxon tribes in the late fifth century but it was Geoffrey of Monmouth,

author of the fictional *History of the Kings of Britain*, who began the legend by transforming Arthur into a king. This King Arthur created the Round Table around which his bravest knights would sit; and people are still trying to locate his capital, Camelot. The legend was revived in the 19th century, through poets such as Lord Tennyson.

CHRISTIANITY

In AD597, a monk called Augustine arrived in England with a mission set by the Pope to convert the English to Christianity. Beginning by converting the King of Kent, Augustine established his headquarters at Canterbury; today, the Archbishop of Canterbury is still head of the Anglican Church.

IF YOU LIKED THIS...
Visit the Great Hall at Winchester, the only surviving part of Winchester Castle. Inside is a round table, said to be Arthur's, although it only dates back to the 13th century.

SAXON KINGS

FIFTH OR SIXTH CENTURY TO AD1066

SEVEN KINGDOMS

In the AD600s, there were seven different kingdoms in England, each one with their own ruler: Wessex, Northumbria, Kent, East Anglia, Mercia, Sussex and Essex.

By the AD860s, England was under attack from the Vikings of Scandinavia, who captured the city of York and launched attacks against the kingdoms of Mercia, East Anglia and Wessex.

KING ALFRED AND HIS SUCCESSORS

By the AD870s, Wessex was the only surviving kingdom. Northumbria, East Anglia and Mercia had all been defeated by the Danes and other kingdoms had lost their status through lack of political ambition. Alfred of Wessex defeated the Danes in Wessex in AD878 and took over London in AD886. He drafted a treaty called Danelaw which gave northern and eastern England to the Danes; and allowed him to take the south and west for himself.

Athelstan, his grandson, later united all of England under his rule and is known as the 'first King of England'. In AD973, his nephew, Edgar, was crowned King of England at Bath Abbey in the first coronation ceremony.

DID YOU KNOW?
Alfred the Great is the only English ruler to be called the 'Great'.

SAXONS V. DANES

One of the weakest Anglo-Saxon kings, Aethelred the Unready (AD968–1016) had constant trouble fighting off the Danish Vikings. After the death of Aethelred and his son Edmund Ironside, King Canute, leader of the Danes, successfully ruled over England for 19 years. A period of disruption followed his death, only coming to an end in 1042, when Aethelred's last surviving son, Edward the Confessor, took over.

WEIRD AND WONDERFUL
King Canute was told by flattering courtiers that he was so powerful he could hold the sea back on his own.

Statue of Alfred the Great

17

EDWARD THE CONFESSOR

BORN: c.1003/4 | **DIED:** 1066 | **REIGNED:** 1042–66
MARRIED: Edith, daughter of Earl of Wessex | **CHILDREN:** died childless

Edward the Confessor had an unsettled early life after King Canute of Denmark overthrew the English royal family. Later, as King of England, he was famous for building Westminster Abbey.

DISINHERITANCE

Edward the Confessor was the younger son of Aethelred the Unready (see p.17) and Emma of Normandy. After the deaths of his father and half-brother, King Canute of Denmark invaded England and became king, marrying Edward's mother. Edward and his brother, Alfred, lived in exile in Normandy until the death of Canute in 1035. A year later, Alfred and Edward led an army into England to regain the throne. This attempt was disastrous, leading to the capture and murder of Alfred. Edward the Confessor finally became king six years later following the death of King Hardicanute, as there was no rival left.

KING OF ENGLAND

Edward was a deeply religious king, leading to his nickname, 'the Confessor'. While he was king, England remained a stable country.

He built the first Westminster Abbey, of which little now remains, as his burial place and in 1045 married Edith, daughter of one of the most powerful earls in the country, Godwin, Earl of Wessex.

 DID YOU KNOW?
Edward the Confessor is the only King of England to have been canonised.

CELIBATE LIFE

Edward the Confessor died without consummating his marriage due to a vow of celibacy. This left him with no heirs, which threw England back into war for most of 1066, with his brother-in-law, Harold II, fighting off invasions from other potential heirs on two different fronts (see p.19).

 IF YOU LIKED THIS...
Visit Westminster Abbey to see the tomb of Edward the Confessor.

Edward the Confessor as shown in the Bayeux Tapestry

HAROLD II

BORN: c.1020/22 | **DIED:** 1066 | **REIGNED:** January to October 1066
MARRIED: Edith, daughter of the Earl of Mercia
CHILDREN: Harold and possibly Ulf, although Ulf may have been Harold II's son by his mistress

Harold II became king by popular choice on the death of his brother-in-law, Edward the Confessor. Faced with war on two fronts, he was killed at the Battle of Hastings (see p.20)

CAPTURE IN NORMANDY

Harold II, Edward the Confessor's brother-in-law, was named king by the Confessor on his deathbed. He accepted the crown and, in so doing, triggered a war.

Two years previously, Harold had been taken prisoner by Duke William of Normandy and he had sworn an oath that on the Confessor's death, he would help William to become King of England.

In addition to the threat from Normandy, in 1065, the Northumbrians had rebelled against Harold's brother, Tostig, Earl of Northumbria. Harold replaced him, making Tostig his bitter enemy.

WAR ON TWO FRONTS

Harold II didn't have to wait long for his enemies to make their move. In September 1066, Harald Hardrada, King of Norway, invaded England for the throne, helped by Tostig. Harold II led his armies to the north of England and defeated them at the Battle of Stamford Bridge, where both Harald Hardrada and Tostig were killed.

This was on 25 September 1066. Three days later, William of Normandy landed at Pevensey, in the south of England. Harold, on hearing this, raced south to deal with this new threat. This proved to be his biggest mistake as it meant that his troops were exhausted going into battle. Harold was defeated and killed by William at the Battle of Hastings. Harold is known as the last Saxon King of England.

DID YOU KNOW?
Harold II was the last English monarch to be defeated by a foreign invader.

Harold II swearing allegiance to William the Conqueror

BATTLE OF HASTINGS

1066, the year of the Battle of Hastings, is one of the most famous in English history. The invading Normans killed the Saxon King of England at Hastings, changing the course of English history forever.

WILLIAM'S ARRIVAL IN ENGLAND

William, Duke of Normandy, arrived in England at Pevensey Beach on 28 September 1066. Apparently, William tripped and fell when he was getting off the boat. His men, taking that as a bad omen, gasped in horror, but William, quick to seize the moment, picked up some sand and said, 'See, my lords, I have taken possession of England with both my hands!' He then led raids into the surrounding countryside, but didn't progress any further, possibly to leave a retreat route clear for him across the sea in case of defeat.

DID YOU KNOW?

The Battle of Hastings wasn't fought at Hastings, but at Senlac Hill, several miles inland.

MEETING OF THE ARMIES

On 13 October 1066, Harold's army set up camp on Senlac Hill, several miles inland. The following day, the battle began. At first, no army could gain power over the other. Both armies had about 7,000 men each. Harold had the advantage of the high position, but the disadvantage of a lack of archers, left behind on the long march south; whereas William's army had both archers and cavalry.

It seemed at first that Harold's army would be able to hold their position, but the Normans tried the trick of pretending that they were giving in and turning away. Harold's army then chased after them to kill them, but suddenly found they were under attack. This badly decimated Harold's army on the ridge.

WILLIAM'S VICTORY

William's final attack came in the evening of the 14 October, after a day of hard fighting. Archers attacked the weakened Saxon defences, killing Harold in

Pevensey Beach where William the Conqueror landed in 1066

the process. Without their leader, the Saxons gave in, leaving William the victor of the field. William refused Harold proper burial on the grounds that he had apparently gone against his oath in promising William the crown, then taking it for himself (see p.19).

IF YOU LIKED THIS...
Visit Bayeux, in Normandy to see the Bayeux tapestry, which depicts the events of the Battle of Hastings. To get a detailed look at a replica of the tapestry, visit www.bayeuxtapestry.org.uk.

Battle Abbey in East Sussex

IF YOU LIKED THIS...
Visit Battle Abbey, on the site of the battlefield. The altar is said to mark the spot of Harold's death.

WILLIAM I: KING OF ENGLAND

William then marched to London, taking first Dover and then Canterbury, on his way. He was crowned king on Christmas Day at Westminster Abbey; as it was the burial place of Edward the Confessor, this emphasised William's right as Edward's successor.

ENGLAND AFTER HASTINGS

There were huge changes in England after the Norman invasion. Saxon nobles lost their lands to Norman barons, who held on to their position by building castles on their territory. William also adopted the feudal system giving his most trusted barons lands and titles in return for their support in times of trouble.

WEIRD AND WONDERFUL
Harold's face was so mutilated, his body could only be identified by his mistress, Edith Swan-Neck.

The Normans

Although the Normans had no claim to the throne of England, they succeeded in conquering England, and ruled over one of the most violent periods of English history through aggression and ruthlessness.

England remained stable under the rules of William I and his sons William II and Henry I, but the country descended into anarchy throughout the reign of his grandson, King Stephen.

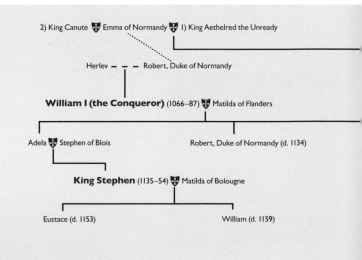

The White Tower at the Tower of London

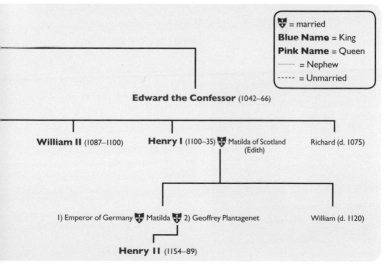

♔ = married
Blue Name = King
Pink Name = Queen
·········· = Nephew
----- = Unmarried

Edward the Confessor (1042–66)

William II (1087–1100)   **Henry I** (1100–35) ♔ Matilda of Scotland (Edith)   Richard (d. 1075)

1) Emperor of Germany ♔ Matilda ♔ 2) Geoffrey Plantagenet   William (d. 1120)

Henry II (1154–89)

23

WILLIAM I THE CONQUEROR

 BORN: 1027/8 | **DIED:** 9 September 1087 | **REIGNED:** 1066–87
MARRIED: Matilda of Flanders | **CHILDREN:** Robert, Richard, Cecilia, Adeliza, William, Constance, Adela, Henry, Agatha, Matilda

William the Conqueror was undoubtedly one of the toughest and most ruthless leaders in English history. His reign was famous for the hated Domesday Book and the building of several defensive fortresses.

BUILDING OF DEFENSIVE CASTLES

William I confirmed his position as king by building a number of fortresses in and around London and throughout England.

One of the most famous is the White Tower of the Tower of London; another is Windsor Castle, later rebuilt in the 12th century.

This policy of castle-building and disciplined armies established William I's position on the throne as a highly skilled military leader.

THE DOMESDAY BOOK

William I ordered the writing of the Domesday Book in 1085 to find out how much land and resources existed in England, and how much they were worth.

A group of men were sent around the country to find out how much property each person had and to assess how much tax they could pay. The book was called the Domesday Book, and it is now one of the main sources for English history of the 11th century.

WILLIAM'S DEATH

William I divided his kingdom amongst his surviving sons, leaving Normandy to Robert; England to William; and five thousand pounds in silver to Henry. The astute Henry ended up being the most powerful of William's sons.

William the Conqueror became the first Norman King of England

 IF YOU LIKED THIS...
Visit the Tower of London, where William's original castle, the White Tower, is still standing.

WILLIAM II

 BORN: c.1056–60 | **DIED:** 2 August 1100 | **REIGNED:** 1087–1100
MARRIED: unmarried | **CHILDREN:** died childless

Although William II (also known as William Rufus) demonstrated his ability to hold onto the crown, he raided monasteries for funds, leading to a tense relationship with the Church.

WARS AGAINST NORMANDY

Rebellions were led against William II's right to be King of England as many felt that his older brother Robert, Duke of Normandy, should have inherited the throne. However, Robert was a weak leader, making it easy for William II to weaken Robert's hold in Normandy. Robert was later imprisoned by his younger brother, Henry I, until his death in 1134 (see p.26).

William II died a mysterious death in the New Forest

WILLIAM II'S RELATIONSHIP WITH THE CHURCH

When William II needed to raise money, he raided monasteries. This made him very unpopular with the Church, and caused conflict with the Archbishop of Canterbury, St Anselm. When St Anselm visited the Pope in Rome in 1097 he left Canterbury unprotected. This gave William II the chance to seize the funds of Canterbury for himself.

NEW FOREST

On 2 August 1100, William II was shot dead while hunting in the New Forest, by his friend Walter Tyrell. There are still rumours that this accident was deliberate murder, on the orders of William's younger brother, Henry.

 DID YOU KNOW?
William II's brother Richard was also killed in the New Forest. At the time people believed that there was a curse on the forest.

As soon as the accident happened, Henry jumped on his horse and started galloping to the royal treasury at Winchester, the ancient capital of the Saxon kings, to stake his claim to the throne. Racing against him was William de Breteuil, a supporter of Robert, Duke of Normandy. Henry reached Winchester first, and succeeded in convincing the crowd that he should take the crown.

HENRY I

BORN: September 1068 | **DIED:** 1/2 December 1135
REIGNED: 1100–35 | **MARRIED:** Matilda (Edith) of Scotland (1100);
Adeliza of Louvain (1121) | **CHILDREN:** Matilda, William

Henry I was known as 'Beauclerc' for his learning and was one of the most able administrators to sit on the throne. His death caused a crisis in the succession, leading to years of civil war.

HENRY AS KING

On Henry I's accession, his older brother Robert, Duke of Normandy, was still alive and claiming the crown of England. The quarrel between them ended in the battle of Tinchebrai in 1106, from which Henry emerged victorious, taking Robert prisoner and keeping him in captivity until Robert's death in 1134.

From that moment, Henry ruled both England and Normandy through a combination of justice and cruelty. On the one hand, he brought back the death penalty for theft and ordered blinding and mutilation for lesser crimes. On the other, he showed no favouritism towards the noble classes: penalties for committing crimes were the same for everyone. He was named the 'Lion of Justice', and England at this time was understandably relatively law-abiding!

WHITE SHIP DISASTER

The worst disaster of Henry I's reign was the death of his only son, William. On 25 November 1120, William was travelling to England on the *White Ship*, when it ran aground and sank, leaving only one survivor.

Henry I was left with only one legitimate child, his daughter Matilda, whom he named as his successor. On his death, however, Matilda's claim to the throne was contested by her cousin, Stephen of Blois, leading to a period of anarchy and rebellion.

DID YOU KNOW?
Henry I's charter on his accession required that justice and mercy should be exercised in all judgments. This has become part of the coronation oath, still sworn by the monarch today.

Henry I, the most successful of the Conqueror's sons

STEPHEN

BORN: 1096/7 | **DIED:** 25 October 1154 | **REIGNED:** 1135–54
MARRIED: Matilda of Boulogne | **CHILDREN:** Eustace, William, Mary

Stephen's reign became a period of upheaval following the peaceful reign of Henry I. He lacked the ability to rule as ruthlessly as his predecessors, and faced constant challenges from his cousin, Matilda.

EARLY YEARS OF STEPHEN'S REIGN

Following the death of Henry I, the next in line to the throne was his only surviving daughter, Matilda. However, her arrogance had already driven away the leading barons of the country; and when Henry I's nephew, Stephen, claimed the crown, they gave him their support.

Previous Norman kings had ruled with a harshness that ensured their firm grip on the crown. Although known for his bravery, Stephen lacked this characteristic. His reign is remembered for constant wars led against him by Matilda (who wanted to regain her crown) and against her son Henry.

STEPHEN V. MATILDA

Matilda lived in France with her second husband, but arrived in England in 1139 to regain the throne, sparking a civil war. For years, she and Stephen fought it out, neither side gaining supremacy. In 1141, Matilda briefly ruled over England, until her arrogance once again annoyed her supporters, leading to Stephen being made king again. This chaos was increased by the barons who used England's descent into civil war for their own purposes, leading raids against

neighbours to gain more land. This period is still known as the 'Anarchy'. With no stable ruler, there was no-one to keep them in line.

In 1153, Stephen's eldest son Eustace had died, and his second son William had no interest in ruling England. Stephen agreed that Matilda's son Henry should succeed him as king after his death, restoring the line of succession.

WEIRD AND WONDERFUL

Stephen was crowned twice, once on becoming king and again on being reinstated in 1141.

Stephen, the least ruthless of the Norman kings

The Plantagenets

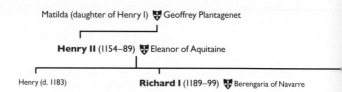

Matilda (daughter of Henry I) 🛡 Geoffrey Plantagenet

Henry II (1154–89) 🛡 Eleanor of Aquitaine

Henry (d. 1183)　　　　　　　　**Richard I** (1189–99) 🛡 Berengaria of Navarre

Edward, the Black Prince (d. 1376) 🛡 Joan of Kent　　　　Lionel, Duke of Clarence
(founder of the House of York,
see p.42)

1) Isabelle of France 🛡 **Richard II** (1377–99) 🛡 2) Anne of Bohemia

Henry II came to the throne after King Stephen agreed to recognise him as his heir. The name 'Plantagenet' is said to come from the *Planta genista* (common broom) plant, which Geoffrey of Anjou, Henry II's father, apparently wore in his hat. The Plantagenet royal family were famous for their energy and courage in battle, making them highly respected and successful monarchs.

Richard the Lionheart on crusade

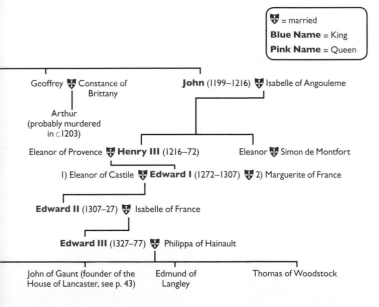

⚜ = married
Blue Name = King
Pink Name = Queen

Geoffrey ⚜ Constance of Brittany

Arthur
(probably murdered
in c.1203)

John (1199–1216) ⚜ Isabelle of Angouleme

Eleanor of Provence ⚜ **Henry III** (1216–72)

Eleanor ⚜ Simon de Montfort

1) Eleanor of Castile ⚜ **Edward I** (1272–1307) ⚜ 2) Marguerite of France

Edward II (1307–27) ⚜ Isabelle of France

Edward III (1327–77) ⚜ Philippa of Hainault

John of Gaunt (founder of the House of Lancaster, see p. 43)

Edmund of Langley

Thomas of Woodstock

HENRY II

BORN: 5 March 1133 | **DIED:** 6 July 1189 | **REIGNED:** 1154–89
MARRIED: Eleanor of Aquitaine | **CHILDREN:** Henry, Matilda, Richard, Geoffrey, Eleanor, Joanna, John

Henry II was one of the most energetic monarchs to rule England. An immensely capable leader, his reign was overshadowed by the murder of the Archbishop of Canterbury and the rebellion of his sons.

HENRY II'S EMPIRE

Henry II's empire stretched from the north of England to the Pyrenees, covering the whole of western France, meaning he owned more territory in France than the French king. Henry II was full of energy, never sleeping more than five hours every night. His temper was legendary, it is said he even foamed at the mouth in a screaming rage, and reduced men to quivering wrecks.

THOMAS BECKET

Thomas Becket was one of Henry II's closest friends, and Henry appointed him the Archbishop of Canterbury in 1161. Criminals often chose to be tried by the Church because of the light sentences handed out. Henry II wanted this changed, and thought Becket would back him up. However, Becket, on becoming Archbishop, decided that his main allegiance was to the Church, and altered nothing. Things became so bad that Henry II allegedly screamed at his surrounding Court, 'Who will rid me of this turbulent priest?'

Four knights took this literally, rode to Canterbury and murdered Thomas Becket in Canterbury Cathedral. Henry II was horrified, and asked priests to beat him with a whip as an act of penance. Thomas Becket was canonised two years after his murder.

PERSONAL LIFE

Henry II married Eleanor of Aquitaine, one of the greatest heiresses in Europe but he soon began a relationship with Rosamund Clifford, thus turning his wife against him. The result was that Eleanor and their sons led a rebellion against Henry II, which Henry initially won. However, worn out by constant family uprisings, his heart broken by the news that his youngest son John had also joined the rebels, Henry died in 1189.

IF YOU LIKED THIS...

Visit Canterbury Cathedral to see the site of Thomas Becket's murder or Fontevraud Abbey in France, where Henry II and his wife Eleanor are buried.

RICHARD I THE LIONHEART

BORN: 8 September 1157 | **DIED:** 6 April 1199 | **REIGNED:** 1189–99
MARRIED: Berengaria of Navarre | **CHILDREN:** died childless

Richard I has gone down in history as the 'Lionheart'. A brave and charismatic military leader, he spent very little time in England, as he regularly led Crusades in the Middle East.

CRUSADES

The Middle East at the time was dominated by Saladin, a great Muslim leader. He took over Jerusalem and removed the King. The Christian leaders of western Europe were appalled, and Richard I immediately left England in 1189 to take up arms against him. The war ended in a truce in 1192, as both sides were exhausted. One condition of the truce was that Christians would be allowed to travel through Jerusalem without being attacked.

Richard I was away from England until 1194, because he was captured on the way back from Jerusalem, by Duke Leopold of Austria. One story has it that Richard I's minstrel, Blondel, located him by singing a song that only he and Richard knew! A more reasonable account is that Richard was freed in return for a ransom being paid.

WEIRD AND WONDERFUL
Richard I only spent 10 months of his 10-year reign in England.

THE SUCCESSION

Richard was killed by an arrow while besieging the Castle of Chalus in France in 1199. The archer who had deliberately aimed at and killed him was flayed alive, proof of the anger and shock felt by his supporters. Dying without an heir, Richard left the empire divided between two possible successors: his nephew, Arthur and his younger brother, John.

IF YOU LIKED THIS...
Visit Fontevraud Abbey in France, where Richard I is buried.

Statue of Richard I

JOHN

BORN: 24 December 1166 | **DIED:** 18–19 October 1216
REIGNED: 1199–1216 | **MARRIED:** Isabella of Gloucester (1189); Isabelle of Angouleme (1200) | **CHILDREN:** (by Isabelle of Angouleme): Henry, Richard, Joanna, Isabella, Eleanor

King John's reign is famous for the loss of territories in France and the treaty of Magna Carta, which reduced the monarchy's power (see p.34). He is also believed to have arranged the murder of his nephew, Arthur.

JOHN V. ARTHUR

When Richard I died, his nephew, Arthur, was next in line. However, Arthur was only 12 years old, and had never been to England. John was an adult, and a better choice from the English barons' point of view. Arthur was captured by John in 1202 and mysteriously vanished. One theory is that John murdered him and dumped his body in the River Seine.

ROBIN HOOD

According to popular legend, Robin Hood was a supporter of Richard the Lionheart, driven to becoming an outlaw by the villainous Sheriff of Nottingham, friend of the future King John, during Richard I's absence. He and his followers were said to inhabit the forest of Sherwood in Nottingham, stealing from the rich to give to the poor.

In reality, several Robin Hoods existed throughout the 13th century as fugitives from the law. In the later 1200s, the Sheriff of Nottingham was fighting several outlaws from Sherwood Forest so it seems likely that the story has some basis in fact.

IF YOU LIKED THIS...
Visit Worcester Cathedral, where King John is buried or make your choice of any Robin Hood film, including *Robin Hood Prince of Thieves* with Kevin Costner as Robin Hood and Alan Rickman as the Sheriff of Nottingham.

Above: King John
Top: The Magna Carta

HENRY III

 BORN: 1 October 1207 | **DIED:** 16 November 1272 | **REIGNED:** 1216–72
MARRIED: Eleanor of Provence | **CHILDREN:** Edward, Margaret, Beatrice, Edmund

Henry III was a devoted family man, but not a brilliant king. His wife and her relatives became hated for their greed, and the barons rebelled against him, leading to a temporary loss of power (see p.35).

MARRIAGE

At the age of 28, Henry III married Eleanor, the daughter of the Count of Provence. It was an extremely happy marriage, but one which almost lost him the crown. Eleanor came to England with several of her relatives, who were quick to encourage the King to give them lands and wealth. Infatuated with Eleanor, Henry III agreed to everything. One of the more famous areas owned by a member of Eleanor's family is the present-day Savoy Hotel in central London. The land it is on was given to Count Peter of Savoy, Eleanor's uncle. Angered by the greed of the King's in-laws, the noblemen rose up against the royal family, almost defeating them (see p.35).

Portrait of Henry III

THE 'BUILDER-KING'

It was Henry III who ordered two walls to be built around the Tower of London and Windsor Castle, for extra defence. Henry III was a great admirer of Edward the Confessor, even naming his eldest son, the future Edward I, after him. The Confessor had built the first Westminster Abbey as his burial place (see p.18), but Henry III ordered it to be made much bigger as a fitting memorial

for the only King of England to be canonised. Westminster Abbey is where Henry III's tomb is now, leading to the tradition of most subsequent medieval kings being buried there.

 WEIRD AND WONDERFUL

Henry III was extremely religious and on his way to meet the King of France, Louis IX he insisted on stopping to pray every time he met a priest. This delayed his arrival so much that Louis banned all priests from his route the next time!

BARONS' REVOLT
AND LOSS OF NORMANDY

The Barons' War in the reign of King John (see p.32) brought about the infamous treaty of Magna Carta. Fifty years later, his son, Henry III, was also faced with a dangerous baronial challenge to his authority.

LOSS OF NORMANDY

In 1189 John angered Philip Augustus, the King of France, by marrying the already betrothed Isabella of Angouleme, leading to France declaring war on John. The French succeeded in recapturing most of the English-controlled territories in France, including Normandy, meaning the English noblemen started to lose confidence in John.

 DID YOU KNOW?
Henry II named his son 'Lackland' because of the difficulty of finding land for him. John's later loss of the French territories seemed to justify that early nickname!

Portrait showing John putting his seal on the Magna Carta

JOHN V. THE BARONS

After John's final defeat in France in 1214 following an attempt to regain his lost lands, a group of barons rose up against him, refusing to grant him more money to carry out further campaigns. In June 1215, they entered London and forced John to agree to a meeting with them. The meeting place was Runnymede, near Windsor, a place still synonymous with the notorious treaty of Magna Carta.

MAGNA CARTA

The Magna Carta is famous for reducing the authority of the monarch. It was drawn up by the barons to lessen the power of the King, asserting the rights of the barons, the Church and the people. One of the most famous clauses in Magna Carta stated that no-one should be imprisoned or punished without going through the proper legal system; until then, the King could imprison or punish anyone he wished.

Forced to put his seal to Magna Carta for his own safety, King John had revoked it less than a year later, causing the barons to bring Prince Louis, the future King of France, into England to become king in John's place. Louis entered London with little resistance and was pronounced king at St Paul's Cathedral, although he was not crowned.

'Let us, therefore, commend our souls to God, for our bodies are theirs!'

Simon de Montfort, on seeing the strength of the royal army at Evesham

Henry III faced further uprisings from the barons

Fighting continued until the death of King John in October 1216. The barons unanimously voted for his nine-year-old son, Henry, as king, and were then faced with the task of telling Louis he was no longer wanted! Following defeat at the Battle of Lincoln in 1217, Louis returned to France.

WEIRD AND WONDERFUL

King John couldn't write, so he didn't sign the Magna Carta; he simply put his seal to it.

THE SECOND BARONS' WAR

John's son, Henry III, also had to deal with a baronial uprising, close to the end of his reign. He was unpopular due to his constant demands for money, and the barons, led by Henry III's brother-in-law, Simon de Montfort, forced him to agree to a further treaty, the Provisions of Oxford, which gave the barons the power to deal with government business.

When Henry III abandoned this treaty, war broke out. The barons won an initial victory at the Battle of Lewes in 1264, where Henry III was taken prisoner.

VICTORY FOR THE ROYALISTS

In 1265 Henry III's son, the future Edward I, also in captivity, escaped and defeated the barons at the Battle of Evesham in 1265, where Simon de Montfort was killed. Royal power had been restored. This period was the closest England came to becoming a republic until the Commonwealth in the 1600s (see p.69).

IF YOU LIKED THIS...

To see the Magna Carta, visit Salisbury Cathedral, Lincoln Cathedral or the British Library where there are original copies of it.

Salisbury Cathedral

EDWARD I

BORN: 17/18 June 1239 | **DIED:** 7 July 1307 | **REIGNED:** 1272–1307
MARRIED: Eleanor of Castile (1254); Marguerite of France (1299)
CHILDREN: Eleanor, Joanna, Margaret, Mary, Elizabeth, Edward, Thomas, Edmund

Edward I was a tough soldier, who fought endless wars with Scotland and Wales during his reign. He was, like his father, a devoted family man; unlike his father, a powerful ruler.

WARS WITH WALES AND SCOTLAND

At the time of Edward's reign, Wales was a separate principality from England. Llywelyn ap Gruffydd, prince of north Wales, didn't attend the coronation of Edward I, and refused to swear allegiance to him, affirming his belief in Welsh independence.

Edward I declared war in 1277, winning a final victory five years later in 1282, when Llywelyn was killed. Llywelyn's brother, Daffyd, originally swore allegiance to Edward I, but went over to the side of his brother. He was captured after Llywelyn's death and in 1283 he became one of the first people in England to be hanged, drawn and quartered for treason. Edward I's son, the future Edward II, was named Prince of Wales; and this has been the title of the heir to the throne ever since.

Edward I is also famous for his wars against Scotland (see p.38).

 IF YOU LIKED THIS...
Visit Caernarfon Castle, where the investiture (the formal recognition of an heir) of each new Prince of Wales takes place.

CHERE REINE OR CHARING CROSS

Edward I was devoted to his first wife, Eleanor of Castile. She died in Lincoln in 1290 and Edward ordered that her body be carried to Westminster Abbey for her burial, and that a cross should be erected at each one of the 12 resting places on the route. Only three original Eleanor crosses now exist, at Waltham Cross, Geddington and Hardingstone.

Edward I being crowned king

EDWARD II

BORN: 25 April 1284 | **DIED:** 21 September 1327 | **REIGNED:** 1307–27
MARRIED: Isabella of France | **CHILDREN:** Edward, John, Eleanor, Joanna

Edward II was the opposite of his father. He lost control of Scotland, and antagonised his wife through his affairs with other men. He was eventually overthrown by his wife and her lover and murdered.

PIERS GAVESTON AND HUGH LE DESPENSER

Edward II met Piers Gaveston in his youth and began an intense love affair with him. In 1312, tired of the influence Gaveston had over the King, the noblemen rose up against him, captured Gaveston and had him beheaded on Blacklow Hill, near Warwick Castle.

Edward II's subsequent favourite, Hugh le Despenser, was much more aggressive and ambitious than Gaveston; he would seize other nobles' lands for himself, encouraged by the King. The situation grew steadily worse until eventually war broke out against Edward II.

THE REBELLION OF ISABELLA AND ROGER MORTIMER

Edward II's wife, Isabella, had been loyal to her husband for years but the situation with the Despenser family brought her to the end of her patience. She took Roger Mortimer, one of the leading barons of the country, as her lover and together, they led a rebellion against Edward II, which was a success.

Edward II was despised after his defeat at the Battle of Bannockburn in Scotland

Edward II being offered the crown

(see p.39) and the Despenser family had ensured his total lack of support. Isabella and Mortimer seized control, and Edward II was locked up in Berkeley Castle and murdered.

Mortimer was later executed on the orders of Edward II's son, Edward III; and Isabella was shut up in a nunnery for the rest of her life.

WEIRD AND WONDERFUL

When Isabella died in 1358, she asked to be buried with the heart of her dead husband at the Franciscan church at Newgate in London.

SCOTTISH WARS

The wars in Scotland during the 13th and 14th centuries went very well for England in the reign of Edward I, but turned out to be a disaster in the reign of his son, Edward II.

DIVIDED SUCCESSION TO THE SCOTTISH THRONE

In 1290, the direct heir to the throne of Scotland, Margaret, granddaughter of King Alexander III of Scotland, died. Edward I was asked to arbitrate between two claimants, the Balliols and the Bruces, both related to the Scottish royal family. Seeing an opportunity, Edward I declared himself overlord of Scotland and chose John Balliol, who became his puppet ruler. War broke out as the Scots were furious at Edward I's high taxes, and his imprisonment of high-ranking Scottish noblemen.

In 1296, Edward I won the war at the Battle of Dunbar and proclaimed himself King of Scotland. John Balliol was imprisoned by the English but was later released. He spent the rest of his life in France, declaring that he never wanted to have anything to do with Scotland again.

WILLIAM WALLACE

One of the leading figures in this war was William Wallace, son of a knight, and a minor landowner in Scotland, who won a decisive victory against Edward I at the Battle of Stirling Bridge in 1297. This only strengthened Edward I's determination, and he defeated Wallace at the Battle of Falkirk the following year. Wallace was captured in 1305, brought to London and was hung, drawn and quartered at Smithfield in central London. He was immortalised in the 1995 film, *Braveheart*.

IF YOU LIKED THIS...
Visit Smithfield in London, where William Wallace was executed – there is a plaque dedicated to him there.

DEATH OF EDWARD I

By the end of his reign, Edward I believed that Scotland was firmly under his rule. However, in 1306, Robert the Bruce rebelled against Edward I by killing a fellow counsellor and naming himself King of Scotland.

Historians believe that Bruce had probably waited until Edward I was an elderly man, making it less dangerous to pick a fight

Edinburgh Castle

with him! Edward I, however, travelled north for another campaign, succeeding in chasing Bruce around Scotland, and capturing his entire family, before Edward died in 1307.

WEIRD AND WONDERFUL

Robert the Bruce was in a cave feeling he would never defeat the English, when he saw a spider trying to swing a thread from one beam to the next. It failed several times, but then succeeded. An inspired Bruce gained courage from this and went out and kept fighting.

BATTLE OF BANNOCKBURN

In the years that followed his uprising Robert the Bruce waged a guerrilla war against the English; and won a resounding victory at the Battle of Bannockburn in 1314. Edward II and his army were forced to retreat, and Bruce's wife and daughter, in captivity since 1306, were released in return for the English nobles that Bruce had captured.

In 1318, the Scots recaptured Berwick, a key town on the border. Even after that, Edward II refused to give up his perceived sovereignty of Scotland, and the war continued.

IF YOU LIKED THIS...

Visit the Bannockburn Heritage Centre near Stirling Castle, on the site of the battlefield.

Memorial to William Wallace in Smithfield, London

DECLARATION OF ARBROATH

In 1320, the Scots sent a letter, the Declaration of Arbroath, to the Pope, stating that Robert the Bruce was their rightful monarch, and re-affirming Scottish independence from England. Four years later, the Pope recognised Bruce as King of an independent Scotland.

When Edward II was overthrown (see p.37), peace was made through the Treaty of Edinburgh in 1328, which recognised Scotland's rulers as independent from England. Robert the Bruce, having spent most of his reign fighting, died a year later, his dream of independence realised.

DID YOU KNOW?

In 1603, Robert the Bruce's descendant, James VI of Scotland, became King of England, uniting both countries.

'We are fighting ... for freedom ... which no honest man gives up but with life itself.'
Declaration of Arbroath

The Plantagenets

EDWARD III

BORN: 13 November 1312 | **DIED:** 21 June 1377 | **REIGNED:** 1327–77
MARRIED: Philippa of Hainault | **CHILDREN:** Edward, Isabel, Joanna, Lionel, John, Edmund, Mary, Margaret, Thomas

Edward III was, like his grandfather, a tough military ruler. He won several victories in France and it was during his reign that the 100 Years War against France began.

100 YEARS WAR

Edward III's mother, Isabella, was a princess of France. When all her brothers died without having any male heirs, Edward III named himself King of France, and declared war in 1337. One of Edward III's main victories in France was the Battle of Crecy in 1346; his great-grandson, Henry V, won an even more decisive victory at Agincourt (see p.47). The wars against France continued until 1453 (see p.48).

DID YOU KNOW?

The 100 Years War actually lasted 116 years (1337–1453).

ORDER OF THE GARTER

The Order of the Garter is the oldest order of chivalry in English history, initiated by Edward III in 1348. The motto of the Order of the Garter is *Honi soit qui mal y pense* ('Shame on he who thinks evil on it'). Edward III allegedly uttered this phrase after a court lady's garter fell off when he was dancing with her, and the whole court started laughing, convinced that he had made it fall!

IF YOU LIKED THIS...

Visit the home of the Order of the Garter in St George's Chapel at Windsor Castle. Foreign royalty are also members of the order including the Emperor of Japan.

THE BLACK DEATH

The Black Death was a virulent plague which arrived in England in the summer of 1348, spreading to Scotland, Wales and Ireland. It died out in 1350, after killing between 30%–45% of the population. The vastly reduced population led to the Peasants Revolt of 1381 (see p.41).

Edward III was a military ruler who won many battles, including the Battle of Crecy

RICHARD II

BORN: 1366/7 | **DIED:** About February 1400
REIGNED: 1377–99 | **MARRIED:** Anne of Bohemia (1382); Isabelle of France (1396) | **CHILDREN:** died childless

Richard II became king when he was only 10 years old. His finest hour was in the Peasants' Revolt of 1381 when he was 14, but he later lost the crown and was murdered.

THE PEASANTS' REVOLT, 1381

The death toll resulting from the Black Death of 1348–50 meant labourers were desperately needed (see p.40). By 1381, the peasants were frustrated by an increased work load with no pay rise. Then in 1380 the Poll Tax raised rents and this proved to be the last straw. 60,000 peasants marched on London, burning down several key buildings, and putting the Tower of London under siege.

Richard II stayed calm, and met with the rebels the following day, at Smithfield. The Mayor of London, infuriated by the aggressive attitude of the peasant leader, Wat Tyler, stabbed him to death. Richard II, to avoid an ugly situation, declared himself the peasants' leader, and persuaded them to disband, bringing the revolt to an end.

DEPOSAL AND DEATH

Throughout the late 1380s, Richard II made the mistake of giving lands and titles to his favourites, causing Richard's enemies, the Lords Appellant, to rise up against the King and execute these favourites. This humiliation was never forgotten by Richard II, who, for revenge, ordered the execution or exile of these noblemen,

Richard II kneels in prayer

and the murder of his uncle, Thomas of Woodstock. He also confiscated the lands of his cousin, the future Henry IV, fearful of his power and popularity. The nobles, led by Henry, rebelled against him, forcing Richard II to abdicate in 1399. He was imprisoned and probably murdered in February 1400 in Pontefract Castle.

 WEIRD AND WONDERFUL
Richard II is allegedly the inventor of the handkerchief; courtiers write that he would wipe his nose on a square piece of cloth!

The Houses of Lancaster and York

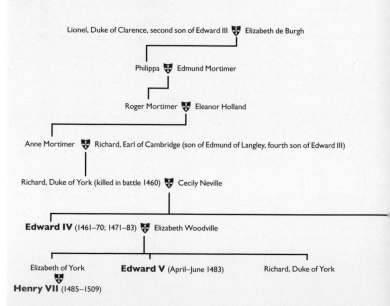

HOUSE OF YORK

Lionel, Duke of Clarence, second son of Edward III — Elizabeth de Burgh

Philippa — Edmund Mortimer

Roger Mortimer — Eleanor Holland

Anne Mortimer — Richard, Earl of Cambridge (son of Edmund of Langley, fourth son of Edward III)

Richard, Duke of York (killed in battle 1460) — Cecily Neville

Edward IV (1461–70; 1471–83) — Elizabeth Woodville

Elizabeth of York

Henry VII (1485–1509)

Edward V (April–June 1483)

Richard, Duke of York

The struggle between the Houses of Lancaster and York can be traced back to the number of sons Edward III had and the murder of Richard II. When Richard II was murdered, power went to his cousin, Henry IV of the House of Lancaster, grandson of Edward III. While Henry IV and his son, Henry V, were stable rulers, Henry VI, the last of the Lancastrian rulers, was not. During Henry VI's reign the House of York rose up against the House of Lancaster in the Wars of the Roses, eventually deposing them. The rival claim of the House of York to the throne came via two of Edward III's sons, Lionel the Duke of Clarence and Edmund of York.

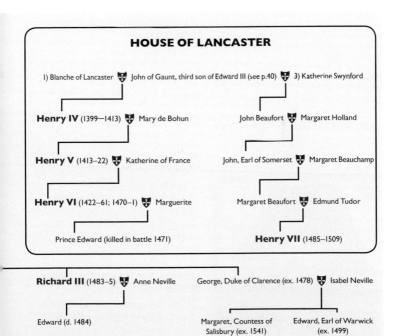

HOUSE OF LANCASTER

1) Blanche of Lancaster 🛡 John of Gaunt, third son of Edward III (see p.40) 🛡 3) Katherine Swynford

Henry IV (1399–1413) 🛡 Mary de Bohun   John Beaufort 🛡 Margaret Holland

Henry V (1413–22) 🛡 Katherine of France   John, Earl of Somerset 🛡 Margaret Beauchamp

Henry VI (1422–61; 1470–1) 🛡 Marguerite   Margaret Beaufort 🛡 Edmund Tudor

Prince Edward (killed in battle 1471)   **Henry VII** (1485–1509)

Richard III (1483–5) 🛡 Anne Neville   George, Duke of Clarence (ex. 1478) 🛡 Isabel Neville

Edward (d. 1484)   Margaret, Countess of Salisbury (ex. 1541)   Edward, Earl of Warwick (ex. 1499)

The Houses of Lancaster and York

HENRY IV

BORN: c.3 April 1367 | **DIED:** 20 March 1413
REIGNED: 1399–1413 | **MARRIED:** Mary de Bohun (1380/1);
Joanna of Navarre (1403) | **CHILDREN:** (by Mary de Bohun): Henry,
Thomas, John, Humphrey, Blanche, Philippa

Henry IV was troubled by guilt after deposing his cousin, Richard II. His reign is famous for the religious persecution of the Lollards and the wars in Wales for Welsh independence.

REBELLIONS AGAINST HENRY IV

By 1403 two rebellions were being led against Henry: one by Owen Glendower for the independence of Wales; the other by the powerful Percy family, the Earls of Northumberland, led by the Earl and his son, Henry Percy, commonly known as Harry 'Hotspur'.

Although Henry Percy was killed in battle in 1403, Owen Glendower had control of most of Wales by 1404. By 1408–9, though, following English victories, most areas that had been recaptured by the Welsh

had again been taken over by the English. Owen Glendower was never captured, and is believed to have died in about 1416.

PERSECUTION OF THE LOLLARDS

The Lollards were a religious group who, like the Protestants 100 years later (see p.60), challenged the beliefs of the Roman Catholic Church. They were given the name 'Lollards' from the Dutch word meaning 'mutter'.

Henry IV, anxious to please the established church because of his unstable position on the throne, supported their stance against the Lollards. In 1401 a statute was passed, ordering that any Lollard who refused to reform would be burned at the stake. This persecution carried on throughout the reign of Henry IV, and in the reign of his son, Henry V.

Portrait of Henry IV

 IF YOU LIKED THIS...
Visit Canterbury Cathedral where Henry IV is the only King of England to be buried or see *Henry IV (Parts 1 and 2)* one of Shakespeare's most famous historical plays.

HENRY V

 BORN: 1386/7 | **DIED:** 31 August/1 September 1422 | **REIGNED:** 1413–22 | **MARRIED:** Katherine de Valois | **CHILDREN:** Henry

Henry V won more decisive victories in France than any other medieval ruler, and was on the point of being named King of France, when he died of dysentery, caused by drinking bad water.

BATTLE OF AGINCOURT

While Prince of Wales, Henry V had shown his military skills in the Welsh wars against Owen Glendower (see p.46). On succeeding to the throne, his main attention was focussed on France, as he was determined to win the French throne, as a continuation of the 100 Years War (see p.40).

Henry V's most famous victory was at the Battle of Agincourt in 1415. This victory was probably due to the technique of the English and Welsh archers, who fired a storm of arrows on the French army. Although exact numbers are not known, it is believed that about 8,000 French were killed, while English losses were only in the hundreds. Henry V then went on to conquer Normandy, a French possession since 1204 (see p.34).

 WEIRD AND WONDERFUL

The insult of sticking the fingers up in a 'V' sign allegedly dates from Agincourt, when French soldiers threatened to cut off the English archers' shooting fingers. On their victory, the English, to show they were still intact, stuck them up in the air!

Henry V at the Battle of Agincourt

MARRIAGE AND DEFEAT OF FRANCE

These victories forced the French to negotiate and in 1420, the Treaty of Troyes was drawn up. The agreement was that Henry V would marry Princess Katherine, daughter of Charles VI, King of France, and that after the death of Charles VI, Henry V and his heirs would inherit the French territory.

Having gained more than any other king during the 100 Years War, Henry V died of dysentery two years later, when his son, Henry VI, was only nine months old.

WARS OF THE ROSES

The Wars of the Roses are the battles between the two rival branches of the royal family: the Houses of York and Lancaster, descended from Edward III (see p.43). The wars lasted for over 30 years and led to the deaths of the majority of the two houses.

Depiction of the Battle of Bosworth Field

HENRY VI: KING OR MONK?

Henry VI was the third King of the House of Lancaster. Although his two predecessors, Henry IV and Henry V, were strong kings, Henry VI was not. He was a very religious man, not at all interested in governing the kingdom; and he consistently appointed the wrong people to power, including the Duke of Somerset, who lost territories in France.

The situation became worse in 1453, when Henry VI had a mental breakdown; this was possibly inherited from his grandfather, Charles the Mad, King of France. His cousin, Richard, Duke of York, head of the House of York, became Lord Protector; but on Henry VI's recovery, and the birth of his son, Richard formed a plan to seize power, leading to a battle for the throne.

DID YOU KNOW?
Henry VI's illness meant that he showed absolutely no response when his only son, Prince Edward, was born, after eight years of marriage; and, when he recovered, had no memory of seeing him before.

CHOOSING SIDES

Allegedly, each side plucked a rose in Temple Gardens in London, to demonstrate who they supported. This scene was dramatised in Shakespeare's *Henry VI*. The Earl of Warwick, at first one of the leading supporters of the House of York, plucked the white rose; the Earl of Suffolk, for the House of Lancaster, plucked a red rose. This is the origin of the name the 'Wars of the Roses'.

IF YOU LIKED THIS...
Visit the gardens of Middle Temple in London to see where the roses were supposedly plucked.

OUTBREAK OF HOSTILITIES

The first battle of the Wars of the Roses was the Battle of St Albans in 1455. While Richard, Duke of York, was the leader of the Yorkist side his opponent was not Henry VI for Lancaster, but Henry VI's wife, Margaret of Anjou. Margaret became become the leader of the Lancastrian side throughout the majority of the wars, particularly on behalf of her son, Prince Edward, heir to the throne. This battle resulted in victory for the House of York, with Henry VI suffering a recurrence of his illness and Richard of York taking over again as Lord Protector.

DEATH OF RICHARD, DUKE OF YORK

A compromise was reached when Henry VI agreed to give the crown to Richard of York and his heirs following his death. However his wife, Margaret, was furious at her son being disinherited, and refused to give in. The Battle of Wakefield, in 1460, was a disaster for the Yorkists, with their leader, Richard, Duke of York, and his second son Edmund, both being killed.

WEIRD AND WONDERFUL

The heads of Richard of York and his son were put up on the Micklegate in the City of York, as a warning to the supporters of the Yorkist cause.

VICTORY FOR EDWARD IV

The eldest son of Richard of York, Edward, carried on fighting, and defeated the Lancastrians at the Battle of Towton in 1461. He was then crowned king in Westminster Abbey.

For nine years, everything went well. However, Edward IV annoyed his main ally, the Earl of Warwick, by marrying Elizabeth Woodville and giving huge amounts of land and power to her family (see p.49). The Earl of Warwick changed his allegiance to the House of Lancaster, leading to a brief period of power for the Lancastrians under Henry VI (1470–1).

St George's Chapel

Edward IV defeated the Lancastrians at the Battle of Barnet, where Warwick was killed. He followed this with an even more decisive victory at the Battle of Tewkesbury, where Prince Edward, heir to Henry VI, was killed. Henry VI was later murdered in the Tower of London (see p.48).

DID YOU KNOW?

The Earl of Warwick was given the title 'the Kingmaker', as he succeeded in putting two different kings on the throne.

LAST BATTLE OF THE WARS OF THE ROSES

The Battle of Bosworth Field is regarded as the last significant battle of the Wars of the Roses, where Richard III of the House of York was killed by Henry VII, descendant of an illegitimate branch of the House of Lancaster (see p.51). Henry VII then married Elizabeth of York, uniting the two houses and ending the war (see p.54).

IF YOU LIKED THIS...

Visit St George's Chapel at Windsor castle. On opposite sides of the chapel are the tombs of the two rivals, Henry VI and Edward IV.

The Houses of Lancaster and York

HENRY VI

 BORN: 6 December 1421 | **DIED:** c.27 May 1471
REIGNED: 1422–61; 1470–71 | **MARRIED:** Marguerite of Anjou
CHILDREN: Edward

Henry VI was a religious king, but also a very weak one. His indecisive reign and the unpopularity of his queen led to the Wars of the Roses, and his eventual capture and murder.

JOAN OF ARC

Upon Henry V's death, France was under English control. However, under the leadership of a peasant girl, Joan of Arc, the city of Orleans was recaptured for the French and Charles VII, the deposed King of France, was crowned at Rheims in July 1429. Joan was later captured and burned at the stake, but the French carried on winning territory back from the English, without much resistance from Henry VI, who wasn't interested in war. By 1453, only Calais was left for the English. This marked the end of the 100 Years War, with victory for the French.

 DID YOU KNOW?
At nine months old, Henry VI is the youngest king to have succeeded to the throne.

JACK CADE'S REBELLION

By 1450, discontent was rising, with the loss of French territories and heavy taxation. A man called Jack Cade led a group of 20,000 men into London, and killed the Treasurer, the Sheriff of

Kent and the Archbishop of Canterbury. The Londoners resisted and succeeded in expelling Cade and his followers. Jack Cade was killed while on the run, and several of his followers were hanged.

 WEIRD AND WONDERFUL
Henry VI is the only King of England to have also been crowned King of France, in 1431.

TWICE DEPOSED AND MURDERED

In 1455, the Wars of the Roses broke out (see p.44). The arrogance of Henry VI's wife, Marguerite of Anjou, who was determined to rule through her weaker husband, had provoked the situation. Overthrown twice in the course of these wars, in 1471 Henry VI was murdered in the Tower of London, believed to have been stabbed to death.

Statue of Henry VI at Eton College

EDWARD IV

BORN: 28 April 1442 | **DIED:** 9 April 1483
REIGNED: 1461–70; 1471–83 | **MARRIED:** Elizabeth Woodville
CHILDREN: Elizabeth, Mary, Cecily, Edward, Richard, Anne, Katherine, Bridget

Edward IV was handsome, charismatic and a brilliant military leader. However, his weakness for women brought about challenges to his throne, and the eventual collapse of the House of York.

MARRIAGE TO A COMMONER

In 1464, Edward IV caused an uproar when he married Elizabeth Woodville, a member of the minor nobility without much money, simply because of her beauty. Her family, delighted by her advancement, were quick to profit by marrying into the nobility. It was the greed of this family that caused Edward IV's chief ally, the Earl of Warwick, to rebel against Edward, leading to his brief deposal in 1470–1 (see p.45).

IF YOU LIKED THIS...

Visit Warwick Castle, home of the Earl of Warwick and one of the largest surviving castles in England.

FAMILY PROBLEMS

Edward IV's younger brother, George, Duke of Clarence, was jealous of his older brother's supremacy and became involved in several plots against him. He even took the part of the Earl of Warwick in the uprising of 1470–1, as Warwick promised him the crown. Later realising that Warwick would never give him the crown George went back to his brother's side. In 1478 it was revealed that George

Edward IV, the most successful Yorkist ruler

was involved in another uprising in Cambridgeshire. He was imprisoned in the Tower of London and murdered; no-one knows how, although rumours state that he was drowned in a butt of malmsey (a sort of fortified Madeira wine).

Edward died in 1483, leaving the throne to his 12-year-old son, Edward V.

DID YOU KNOW?

Edward IV was described as a handsome king who had an infamous reputation as a womanizer and had many mistresses.

EDWARD V

BORN: November 1470 | **DIED:** possibly September 1483
REIGNED: April–June 1483 | **MARRIED:** unmarried | **CHILDREN:** none

Edward V became king at the age of 12 years old. Declared illegitimate, he reigned for only two months, and was probably murdered, with his younger brother, in the Tower of London in 1483.

KING OF ENGLAND?

After the death of his father, Edward IV, Edward V was staying in the Tower of London to prepare for his coronation. Two months later, however, the Bishop of Bath and Wells revealed that Edward IV had secretly been pre-contracted (engaged to be married) to another woman at the time of marrying his wife, Elizabeth Woodville.

This was a disaster for Edward V. As a pre-contract was as binding as marriage, it meant that all the children born to Edward IV and Elizabeth Woodville were declared illegitimate and that Edward had no right to be king. As a result of this, their uncle, Richard III, was crowned instead.

DID YOU KNOW?

Edward V inherited the throne at the age of 12 but he was never officially crowned.

PRINCES IN THE TOWER: MEDIEVAL MURDER MYSTERY

The fate of Edward V and his younger brother Richard is unknown.

The last time they were seen was in the Tower in August 1483; after that, they vanished. They are believed to have been murdered; possibly on the orders of Richard III, so they wouldn't be a focus for any future rebellions.

WEIRD AND WONDERFUL

200 years after the princes disappeared, two skeletons were found in the White Tower of the Tower of London. Believed to be those of the missing boys, they were reinterred in Westminster Abbey.

Another suspect was the future Henry VII, the head of the Tudor family (see p.54). His motive was to get rid of any other claimants to the throne, as his own claim was based on very shaky ground. To this day, no-one knows for sure what exactly happened to them.

IF YOU LIKED THIS...

Visit the Bloody Tower in the Tower of London, where the Princes were said to have been murdered. You can even vote on the identity of the murderer.

1399–1485

RICHARD III

 BORN: 2 October 1452 | **DIED:** 22 August 1485 | **REIGNED:** 1483–5
MARRIED: Anne Neville | **CHILDREN:** Edward (d. 1484)

Richard III's reign has been overshadowed by the question of whether or not he ordered the murder of his nephews. He was killed in battle after only two years on the throne.

FROM LORD PROTECTOR TO KING OF ENGLAND

Until Edward IV's death, Richard III had been based in the north, controlling that area of the country. On Edward's death, Richard was named Lord Protector, to rule England until his nephew, the 12-year-old Edward V, was old enough to take over. When it was revealed, though, that Edward V had no claim to the throne, as his parents were never properly married (see p.50), Richard III took over. Two years later, he was killed at the Battle of Bosworth Field, by the armies of the claimant to the throne, Henry Tudor (see p.45).

Richard III, one of England's most controversial rulers

 IF YOU LIKED THIS...
Visit the Richard III Museum in York.

 WEIRD AND WONDERFUL
Richard III was said by Shakespeare to have a 'hunched back and a withered arm'; in reality he didn't but this legend has persisted through the ages.

In his play William Shakespeare accused Richard III not only of these murders, but of several others as well. Today there is a society dedicated to Richard III, who aim to restore his name. Historians today are still debating the issue.

 DID YOU KNOW?
Richard III was the last English monarch to die in battle.

RICHARD III: SAINT OR SINNER?

There is still huge debate as to whether or not Richard III was guilty of the murder of his nephews, Edward V and his younger brother, the two Princes in the Tower (see p.50).

The Tudors

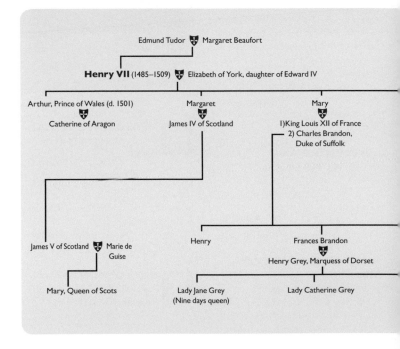

Edmund Tudor ♦ Margaret Beaufort

Henry VII (1485–1509) ♦ Elizabeth of York, daughter of Edward IV

Arthur, Prince of Wales (d. 1501)
♦
Catherine of Aragon

Margaret
♦
James IV of Scotland

Mary
1)King Louis XII of France
2) Charles Brandon,
Duke of Suffolk

James V of Scotland ♦ Marie de Guise

Henry

Frances Brandon
♦
Henry Grey, Marquess of Dorset

Mary, Queen of Scots

Lady Jane Grey
(Nine days queen)

Lady Catherine Grey

Henry VII's right to the throne was highly tenuous. He only became king after killing Richard III in battle (see p.45), and marrying Elizabeth of York, thus uniting the Houses of Lancaster and York and bringing the Wars of the Roses to an end. Despite this the Tudors are among the most outstanding rulers in English history. On the whole, they were tough monarchs, managing to keep the country fairly stable throughout religious upheaval and rebellions from claimants to the throne.

A representation of Henry VIII's court

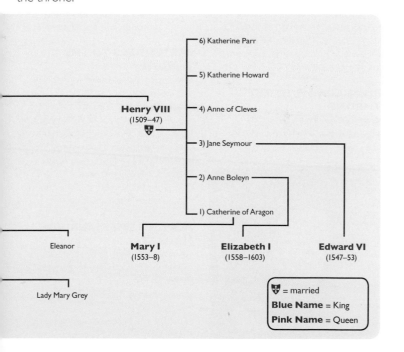

6) Katherine Parr

5) Katherine Howard

Henry VIII
(1509–47)

4) Anne of Cleves

3) Jane Seymour

2) Anne Boleyn

1) Catherine of Aragon

Eleanor

Mary I
(1553–8)

Elizabeth I
(1558–1603)

Edward VI
(1547–53)

Lady Mary Grey

= married
Blue Name = King
Pink Name = Queen

HENRY VII

BORN: 28 January 1457 | **DIED:** 21 April 1509
REIGN: 1485–1509 | **MARRIED:** Elizabeth of York
CHILDREN: Arthur, Margaret, Henry, Mary

Henry VII became King of England through conquest rather than right of birth. His reign was notable for people laying claim to his throne, and for his love of money.

EARLY LIFE

Henry VII's early life was fraught with difficulties. As a member of the House of Lancaster, he left England at the age of 12, due to the continual wars between Lancaster and York, and didn't return until his mid-20s to lay claim to the throne. Henry's defeat of Richard III at the Battle of Bosworth Field led to his accession to the throne.

RIVAL CLAIMS TO THE THRONE

When Henry VII became king, there were more than 18 people alive who had a better claim than he did, due to his descent from two illegitimate lines (see p.45). Several of these claimants were executed in Henry's reign, including the Earl of Warwick, nephew of Edward IV; and John of Gloucester, illegitimate son of Richard III. This policy established the Tudors as undisputed rulers of England.

PRETENDERS TO THE THRONE

After Henry VII's accession, various pretenders laid claim to the throne, stating that they were members of the Yorkist royal family. Lambert Simnel, pretending to be the Earl of Warwick, Edward IV's nephew, was defeated and put into the royal kitchens as a spit-turner. Perkin Warbeck, claiming that he was Richard, Duke of York, the younger of the two Princes in the Tower, was hanged.

PLAYING THE MARRIAGE MARKET

Henry VII's marriage to Elizabeth of York strengthened his position as ruler; he carried on this policy of clever match-making amongst his four children.

His eldest son, Prince Arthur, married Catherine of Aragon, Princess of Spain (see p.58), but died soon after.

Henry VII was a very able and ruthless king

Elizabeth of York, Henry's wife

possible to secure his position. One particular brainwave was a policy from John Morton, Archbishop of Canterbury, which made no-one exempt from paying taxes. On the one hand, if you were seen to be spending a lot of money, you were obviously rich, so were ordered to give some to the King. On the other hand, if you didn't spend a lot of money, you must have some saved, so were still ordered to give some to the King. This policy was nicknamed 'Morton's Fork', as there was no way to get out of it!

By the time Henry VII died, he had left a highly wealthy exchequer and stable country to his son, Henry VIII.

Catherine was then promised to Prince Henry (see p.58), to maintain the Spanish alliance. Princess Margaret married the King of Scotland, and his youngest child, Princess Mary, later married the King of France. Henry VII, like most other rulers, used his children to gain as many allies as possible.

DID YOU KNOW?
Elizabeth of York is the only Queen of England who was also the daughter of a King of England (Edward IV), the sister of a King of England (Edward V), the niece of a King of England (Richard III), the wife of a King of England (Henry VII) and the mother of a King of England (Henry VIII)!

MONEY
Throughout his reign, Henry VII was intent on making as much money as

IF YOU LIKED THIS...
Visit Westminster Abbey to see Henry VII's Chapel, famous for its fan-vaulted roof, which contains the tomb of Henry VII and his wife.

Westminster Abbey where Henry VII is buried

'In government he was shrewd and prudent, so that no-one dared to get the better of him through deceit or guile.'
From *Anglica Historia*

HENRY VIII

BORN: 28 June 1491 | **DIED:** 28 January 1547 | **REIGN:** 1509–1547
MARRIED: Catherine of Aragon (1509); Anne Boleyn (1533);
Jane Seymour (1536); Anne of Cleves (1540); Catherine Howard (1540);
Katherine Parr (1543) | **CHILDREN:** Edward, Mary, Elizabeth

Henry VIII is famous primarily for having six wives (see p.58 for more), but his reign is also significant for a number of other events, making him one of the most famous rulers of England.

EARLY LIFE AND REIGN

When Henry VIII became king in 1509, he was the picture of an ideal monarch. He was 17 years old, handsome and athletic; so athletic, in fact, that he could vault onto the back of a horse wearing full body armour! He left a lot of the governing to his chief minister, Cardinal Wolsey, as he was more interested in being a military hero than getting involved in affairs of state.

Henry had a constant desire to prove himself in battle, and declared war on France in 1512. His most famous victories, though, came closer to home, in his wars against Scotland; establishing him as a significant military presence.

> **'If a lion knew his own strength, hard were it for any man to rule him.'**
> *Sir Thomas More's prophetic quote about Henry VIII when he was a young man*

RELIGIOUS CHANGE

Less than 20 years after his accession, Henry VIII was desperate to get an annulment from his first wife as she had failed to provide him with a son and heir to inherit the throne (see p.58 for more on Henry's wives). As head of the Catholic Church, the Pope was the only person who could authorise an annulment, but he refused and so Henry took matters into his own hands. Although he remained Catholic, he named himself head of the Church of England, completely rejecting the authority of the Pope.

DISSOLUTION OF THE MONASTERIES

Henry's break with Rome led to the Dissolution of the Monasteries. Monasteries all over England were shut down and their wealth was seized by the King as Henry was desperate for

Portrait of Henry VIII dating from 1537

Hampton Court Palace

DID YOU KNOW?
Henry VIII's doctors were afraid to tell him he was dying, because the Treason Act forbade anyone from predicting the death of a king.

Although Henry VIII was desperate to have a healthy son to inherit the crown, it was, ironically, his daughter Elizabeth I, who would go on to continue the strong Tudor reign.

IF YOU LIKED THIS...
Try visiting Hampton Court Palace, one of Henry VIII's chief surviving residences, where his fifth wife was arrested. It is also worth visiting the Tower of London, the site where two of Henry's wives were executed, and home to a display of Henry's armour, as well as one of the heavy guns previously on his flagship, the *Mary Rose*.

money after all his wars. Monks who were adamant that the Pope was the head of the church were frequently captured and executed. This caused religious turmoil, with rebellions being led against Henry VIII, and threats from the French and Spanish rulers, who still supported the Pope.

NAVAL POWER

When Henry VIII became king, the Royal Navy consisted of only five ships. By the time he died, the total number of ships came to well over 50. Henry was the first ruler to fit rows of heavy guns on the side of his ships, all able to fire at once. This development of the Navy led to England becoming a significant power at sea, more able to defend itself from invading forces.

LATER LIFE

By the time he died in 1547, Henry was very overweight and could barely walk, following a jousting accident. He became more and more bad-tempered and ill until his death in January 1547.

Henry VIII's armour is on display in the Tower of London

HENRY VIII'S SIX WIVES

Henry VIII's wives are six of the most famous queens in English history. Henry had several wives for a variety of reasons, but undoubtedly the main one was linked with his obsession to have a healthy son and heir to inherit the throne.

CATHERINE OF ARAGON

Catherine was the youngest child of King Ferdinand and Queen Isabella of Spain. In 1501 she was sent to England to marry Henry's older brother, Arthur. However, Arthur died suddenly only five months later. To maintain the relationship with Spain, Catherine was later betrothed to Henry and they married in 1509.

By 1527, Henry was growing more and more frustrated that he had no son to inherit the throne, as Catherine had given birth to only one daughter, the future Mary I. Henry became very attracted to one of Catherine's ladies-in-waiting, Anne Boleyn; and, convinced that Anne could give him a son, he began to ask the Pope for an annulment from Catherine so that he could marry Anne.

After the Pope's constant refusals, Henry named himself Head of the Church of England and granted himself his own annulment. Catherine always maintained that she was Henry's wife, until her death in 1536.

IF YOU LIKED THIS...
Visit Peterborough Cathedral to see Catherine's grave.

ANNE BOLEYN

Henry's marriage to Anne Boleyn was long-awaited, but it turned out to be a disaster. Anne, like Catherine, also only gave him one daughter (the future Elizabeth I) and had, in addition, a strong, dominating personality, frequently causing Henry to lose his temper. At the end of three years, Henry had completely tired of Anne, and made up a charge of adultery, incest and high treason against her, leading to her execution at the Tower of London in 1536.

WEIRD AND WONDERFUL

Anne Boleyn supposedly had a sixth finger on one of her hands; she invented the hanging sleeve to conceal it.

JANE SEYMOUR

Jane Seymour, lady in waiting to Anne Boleyn, and Henry VIII were betrothed within 24 hours of Anne's execution. A religious conservative, Jane once begged Henry VIII to leave some small monasteries standing, during the Dissolution. Henry lost his temper and reminded her of the fate of Anne Boleyn. Understandably, she never tried to influence him again.

In 1537 Jane died in childbirth giving Henry the son he so desperately wanted (the future Edward VI). For that reason, she was the wife Henry always loved the most.

DID YOU KNOW?
Jane is the only one of Henry's wives buried alongside him, at St George's Chapel in Windsor Castle.

ANNE OF CLEVES

For his fourth wife, Henry VIII married a German princess, Anne of Cleves, to strengthen his links in Europe. Although he hadn't met her in person before agreeing to the marriage, he absolutely loved the portrait that had been painted of her. Unfortunately, the real Anne failed, in Henry's opinion, to match the portrait. He disliked her so much that he annulled the marriage, declaring that he had been unable to consummate it. Anne was given a generous settlement and lived quietly in the country until her death in 1557.

KATHERINE HOWARD

Katherine was Anne Boleyn's first cousin and 30 years younger than Henry when they married. A year after their marriage, whispers started spreading around the Court saying that Katherine was unfaithful. When there was enough evidence of her relationship with another man, she was accused of adultery, arrested and beheaded at the Tower of London in 1542.

DID YOU KNOW?
Three of Henry's wives were ladies-in-waiting to a previous wife!

KATHERINE PARR

Understandably, Henry VIII's sixth wife, a noblewoman called Katherine Parr, had no wish to marry him at all, with the ghosts of two wives who had been beheaded before her. However, as he was king, she couldn't refuse him, and they married in 1543. After Henry's death, four years later, she married again, to Thomas Seymour (the brother of Jane, Henry's third wife) but died in childbirth in 1548.

IF YOU LIKED THIS...
Visit Sudeley Castle to visit Katherine's tomb.

Sudeley Castle, where Katherine Parr is buried

EDWARD VI

BORN: 12 October 1537 | **DIED:** 6 July 1553 | **REIGN:** 1547–53
MARRIED: unmarried | **CHILDREN:** died childless

Edward VI died at the age of just 15, but during his short reign the first prayer book in English was authorised and his religious beliefs led him to alter the line of succession.

LORD PROTECTORS

Edward VI was nine when he became king, and so he had Protectors who ruled for him. One of them, his uncle, the Duke of Somerset, was executed on made-up charges of treason, as other ruthless statesmen wanted his power. Edward issued this order without showing any emotion and he wrote in his diary that Somerset 'had his head cut off upon Tower Hill between eight and nine o'clock in the morning'; his character could be rather cold.

Edward VI's youth meant protectors ruled for him

RELIGION

During Edward's reign, the war between two opposing religions, Protestantism and Catholicism, was showing no signs of abating. In the 1520s, the newly founded Protestant religion challenged the supremacy of the Catholic Church, leading to religious wars that lasted for more than a century.

Edward showed himself to be a very firm believer in the Protestant religion, which caused a rift with his elder half-sister, Mary, who was a staunch Catholic. On his deathbed, although Mary was next in line to become monarch, he was persuaded by his leading councillor, the Duke of Northumberland, to put a Protestant member of the royal family on the throne after him – his cousin, Lady Jane Grey. The Duke of Northumberland's motive was power – Jane was only 15, and married to his son; so his aim was to rule through them. This change in succession left the country divided following Edward's death in 1553.

DID YOU KNOW?

When Edward was a child, his father, Henry VIII, ordered that Edward's rooms be swept and cleaned twice a day, and that all his food be tested for poison, to increase his chances of surviving childhood.

MARY I

BORN: 18 February 1516 | **DIED:** 17 November 1558
REIGN: 1553–58 | **MARRIED:** Philip II, future King of Spain
CHILDREN: died childless

Mary I, Henry VIII's older daughter, was the first queen of England in her own right. Her reign is known for her unhappy marriage and the persecution she led against people of the Protestant religion.

A RIVAL QUEEN: LADY JANE GREY

Lady Jane Grey became queen after Edward VI named her his successor. She reigned for only nine days, before supporters of Mary I took over, and imprisoned her in the Tower of London. She was beheaded there at the age of just 16.

PHANTOM PREGNANCY

In 1554, Mary I married Philip of Spain, heir to the Holy Roman Emperor, Charles V. She was devoted to him, but he had very little affection for her. Shortly after Mary I married Philip, she showed signs of being pregnant. However, although her stomach had swollen up, and she looked as though she was about to give birth at any moment, no baby appeared. The humiliation was appalling for her. It is believed she probably had a stomach tumour, which is why it was swollen.

Mary I, later known as Bloody Mary

religion in England, and turn people back to Catholicism.

However, people were horrified by these executions, and the result was that more and more people turned to Protestantism out of protest. Mary I was given the name 'Bloody Mary' because of this.

RELIGIOUS PERSECUTION

In Mary's reign, she burned over 300 Protestants alive at the stake. A devout Roman Catholic, she believed that Protestants were mistaken in their beliefs, and would go to hell when they died. Her aim was to stamp out the Protestant

IF YOU LIKED THIS...
Visit Smithfield in London and the Martyrs' Memorial in Oxford, where Protestants were burned alive; or Framlingham Castle, in Suffolk, where Mary learnt she was Queen.

ELIZABETH I

BORN: 7 September 1533 | **DIED:** 24 March 1603
REIGN: 1558–1603 | **MARRIED:** unmarried | **CHILDREN:** died childless

Elizabeth I, the younger daughter of Henry VIII, was one of the smartest rulers in history. She never married, and her reign saw explorers travelling the world and a triumphant military victory against Spain.

EARLY YEARS

Following the execution of her mother, Anne Boleyn, Elizabeth was declared illegitimate and barred from the line of succession, although later reinstated by her father, Henry VIII.

Her life became extremely hazardous during the reign of her elder half-sister, Mary I. At the age of only 20, she was imprisoned in the Tower of London, believed by Mary to be involved in a plot to kill her. Elizabeth was clever enough to outwit her accusers, and be released unharmed.

Elizabeth I in one of her elaborate gowns

DID YOU KNOW?
Elizabeth I was very vain, and her wardrobe was rumoured to contain more than 3,000 gowns on her death.

MARY, QUEEN OF SCOTS

Mary, Queen of Scots was the granddaughter of Margaret Tudor (see p.52) and was next in line to become England's ruler if Elizabeth I died childless. However, she was accused of being involved in the murder of her second husband, Lord Darnley, and made things worse when she married the man believed to be behind the murder,

Lord Bothwell. Forced to flee Scotland she was kept captive in England by Elizabeth I where she became involved in several plots to kill Elizabeth so she could become Queen. Her involvement in these plots led to her execution in 1587.

WEIRD AND WONDERFUL
Elizabeth I felt so guilty about ordering the execution of an anointed queen, Mary Queen of Scots, that she pretended her secretary had slipped the death warrant in amongst some other papers for her to sign, and that she hadn't noticed what it was!

EXPLORERS

During the Elizabethan age, explorers were sailing and trading across the world. Two of the most famous explorers during this period were Sir Francis Drake, the first Englishman to circumnavigate the globe, and Sir Walter Raleigh, who allegedly brought tobacco and the potato back to England. They regularly attacked Spanish ships and brought home treasure for the queen, who, although she publicly disassociated herself from their actions, always accepted it!

Replica of the Globe theatre

DID YOU KNOW?

When Elizabeth's favourite, Sir Walter Raleigh, secretly married Bess Throckmorton, Elizabeth's lady-in-waiting, she was so furious that she imprisoned them both in the Tower of London.

THE SPANISH ARMADA

In the summer of 1588, Philip II of Spain, Elizabeth's ex-brother-in-law, sent an Armada to invade England. One reason for this was religion. Elizabeth was Queen of a Protestant country, and Philip II was Catholic. Another reason was the Spanish treasure Elizabeth's sailors kept looting. The Armada was defeated, partly because of bad weather conditions, and partly because the English fleet used fire ships as a weapon (fire ships were empty ships packed with wood and set alight to make them infernos). When they were sent among the Spanish fleet, they broke it apart. This was Elizabeth's most triumphant victory.

ELIZABETHAN THEATRE

It was in Elizabeth's reign that the first purpose-built theatres were created. The most famous playwright in Elizabeth's reign was William Shakespeare, whose plays include *Macbeth*; another was Christopher Marlowe, author of *Dr Faustus*. Elizabeth loved the theatre and often asked plays to be performed for special occasions. *Twelfth Night* by Shakespeare was written for the Court at Christmas.

IF YOU LIKED THIS...

Visit the replica of the Globe Theatre in London, where 16th century plays are performed or Hatfield House, where Elizabeth learnt of her accession.

'I may have the body of a weak and feeble woman, but I have the heart and stomach of a king.'
Elizabeth I's speech to the troops on their way to fight the Armada

The Stuarts

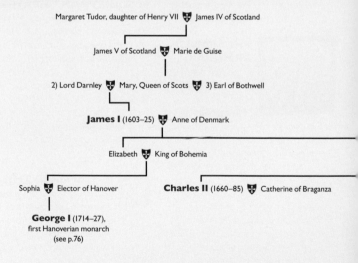

Margaret Tudor, daughter of Henry VII 🛡 James IV of Scotland

James V of Scotland 🛡 Marie de Guise

2) Lord Darnley 🛡 Mary, Queen of Scots 🛡 3) Earl of Bothwell

James I (1603–25) 🛡 Anne of Denmark

Elizabeth 🛡 King of Bohemia

Sophia 🛡 Elector of Hanover

George I (1714–27),
first Hanoverian monarch
(see p.76)

Charles II (1660–85) 🛡 Catherine of Braganza

James VI of Scotland was the great-grandson of James IV and Margaret Tudor, and when Elizabeth I, the last of Henry VIII's children, died childless, he became James I of England. The Stuarts were known for their good looks and charm, but their ability to rule wasn't always as effective. Throughout this period the monarchy lost a good deal of its power, coming to a head in the Civil War of the 1640s.

The Great Fire of London in 1666 destroyed the capital during Charles II's reign

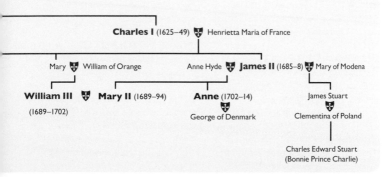

= married
Blue Name = King
Pink Name = Queen

Charles I (1625–49) Henrietta Maria of France

Mary William of Orange

Anne Hyde **James II** (1685–8) Mary of Modena

William III **Mary II** (1689–94)
(1689–1702)

Anne (1702–14)
George of Denmark

James Stuart
Clementina of Poland

Charles Edward Stuart
(Bonnie Prince Charlie)

JAMES I

 BORN: 19 June 1556 | **DIED:** 27 March 1625 | **REIGNED:** 1603–25
MARRIED: Anne of Denmark
CHILDREN: Henry, Elizabeth, Charles

The kingdoms of England and Scotland were united by James, as James VI of Scotland and James I of England. Like the Tudor monarchs, his reign was marked by religious divisions, culminating in the Gunpowder Plot.

KING OF SCOTLAND

James VI of Scotland was crowned King of Scotland at the age of one, after his mother, Mary, Queen of Scots, was forced to abdicate. His childhood was very unsettled with Scotland being ruled by a series of regents, several of whom were murdered by rivals. When he was 21, his mother was beheaded on Elizabeth I's orders (see p.62).

In 1603 Elizabeth I died and James VI of Scotland also became James I of England, uniting the two kingdoms.

James VI of Scotland became James I of England

 DID YOU KNOW?
James I always wore padding inside his clothes to protect him from an assassin's dagger.

GUNPOWDER PLOT

The official religion at the time was Protestantism. In 1605, a group of Catholics, tired of paying fines and disappointed at James I's policy of non-tolerance, plotted to blow up Parliament on 5 November, the day when James I was due to open Parliament. Guy Fawkes has become the most famous of these plotters as it was his job to light the gunpowder. The plot was discovered before it could be carried out and those who were caught alive were hung, drawn and quartered.

MALE FAVOURITES

James I was well-known for picking favourites amongst his male courtiers. Two of the most famous were the Earl of Somerset and the Duke of Buckingham. Neither had titles before James noticed them! Although Buckingham stayed high in the King's favour, Somerset's wife, Frances Howard, was accused of murdering Sir Thomas Overbury, who had been against the marriage; the scandal resulted in them both being banished from Court.

CHARLES I

BORN: 19 November 1600 | **DIED:** 30 January 1649
REIGNED: 1625–49 | **MARRIED:** Henrietta-Maria of France
CHILDREN: Charles, Mary, James, Elizabeth, Henry, Henrietta

Charles I was a well-known patron of the arts, but his stance towards Parliament and religious issues contributed to the Civil War which lost him his throne and his life (see p.68).

CHILDHOOD

Charles I's childhood was one of ill-health: he suffered from weak ankles, probably due to rickets; and had a speech defect, which later improved, although he always had a slight stammer. When Charles was 12, his popular older brother Henry died, leaving Charles as the heir to the throne.

PATRON OF THE ARTS

Charles I was interested in the arts all his life, and added significantly to the Royal Collection of art work, still owned by the royal family today. Charles I was only about 5'3'' tall and always wanted to disguise his lack of height. Several portraits, mainly by Sir Antony Van Dyck, show him on horseback, to make him look taller.

 IF YOU LIKED THIS...
Visit the National Gallery or the National Portrait Gallery which contain some of the portraits of Charles I by Van Dyck.

MARRIAGE AND RELIGION

Charles I's inability to co-operate with Parliament (see p.68) and continuing religious quarrels stored up trouble. By the time Charles I became king, England was a Protestant country and the Catholic Gunpowder Plot of 1605 was still a recent memory (see p.66). Charles favoured the High Anglican style of worship (regarded as being too close to Catholicism because of its elaborate rituals) and his marriage to a devoutly Catholic French princess, Henrietta-Maria, was also unpopular. His attempts to install religious conformity throughout England and Scotland led to war with Scotland, who regarded the new prayer book as being both Catholic and English. This brought about the Civil War of the 1640s (see p.68).

Statue of Charles I

CIVIL WAR

The 1640s saw Civil War waged between the monarchy and the people, led by Parliament. This conflict eventually resulted in the execution of Charles I. For more than a decade afterwards, England was ruled by Parliament, under the leadership of Oliver Cromwell.

Battle of Naseby in 1645

CAUSES OF THE CIVIL WAR

Charles I believed in the Divine Right of Kings, that a king was appointed by God, and so should answer to no-one else. Parliament didn't agree and the constant clashes between King and Parliament led to Charles I closing Parliament for 11 years, between 1629 and 1640. One of these clashes was based on religion: Charles I's beliefs were those of the high church whereas Parliament was of the low church, believing in a simpler way of worship (see p.67).

By 1642, the relationship between King and Parliament had become a terrible one. Charles I needed money to fight a war with Scotland (see p.67) and Parliament forced him to agree to all of their demands before they would give him the funds. Their threat to deprive Charles I of control over the army proved to be the last straw.

On 4 January 1642, Charles I entered the House of Commons with a troop of soldiers to arrest five members of Parliament: Pym, Hampden, Holles, Strode and Sir Arthur Haselrig, but they had already been warned and had fled. Charles I realised that the situation was beyond repairing and left London less than a week later to raise an army against Parliament, marking the start of Civil War.

KING V. PARLIAMENT

The first battle, Edgehill, in October 1642, was inconclusive; but the Parliamentary army won significant victories at the Battle of Marston Moor (1644) and Naseby (1645), through the New Model Army, created by Oliver Cromwell, one of the Parliamentary leaders.

One of the features of the New Model Army was to promote people because of their skill, not because of their family connections, or the amount of money they had.

By 1646, Charles I had lost the war and the political situation was disastrous. Outbreaks of violence against Parliament from Royalist factions convinced Parliament that Charles I had to be removed to restore stability.

DID YOU KNOW?
Ever since Charles I tried to arrest the five members of Parliament, no monarch has been allowed inside the House of Commons.

EXECUTION OF A KING

Charles I was tried in Westminster Hall, part of the modern-day Houses of Parliament. He refused to say a word in his own defence, as he still believed that he should answer to no-one except God. Charles I was judged to be a traitor, and was executed outside the Banqueting House of Whitehall Palace, on 30 January 1649.

WEIRD AND WONDERFUL
Charles I wore two shirts for his execution. He didn't want to shiver with the cold, and make people think he was shivering because he was afraid.

IF YOU LIKED THIS...
Visit Westminster Hall in the Houses of Parliament where Charles I was tried and the Banqueting House, the only surviving part of the palace of Whitehall, where he was beheaded.

OLIVER CROMWELL AND THE COMMONWEALTH

Oliver Cromwell was one of the 59 Parliamentarians who signed the death warrant of Charles I. Following Charles' execution, Cromwell and Parliament took charge of England, creating a system called the Commonwealth. Cromwell established military control over Ireland and was responsible for the massacres at Drogheda and Wexford. On his return, he defeated Royalist forces in Scotland, and later defeated Charles II at the 1651 Battle of Worcester (see p.70). By this time, he had been appointed commander-in-chief of the Parliamentary forces.

In 1653, Cromwell was named Lord Protector, official head of state. He was offered the crown in 1657, but refused it.

It was on Cromwell's death in 1658 that the foundations were laid for Charles II's return to England, and the restoration of the monarchy.

Statue of Oliver Cromwell

CHARLES II

BORN: 29 May 1630 | **DIED:** 6 February 1685
REIGNED: 1660–85 | **MARRIED:** Catherine of Braganza
CHILDREN: died with no legitimate children

The reign of Charles II, Charles I's son, saw the Great Fire of London and religious upheaval; yet Charles II, unlike his father, kept a firm hold on the throne until his death.

RESTORATION

During the Commonwealth, Charles II tried to regain his throne at the Battle of Worcester in 1651. He was defeated but managed to escape. After the death of Oliver Cromwell in 1658, England was leaderless. Charles II produced a declaration saying he would pardon his enemies and defer to Parliament on difficult questions. Following this declaration he was restored to the throne in 1660.

Portrait of Charles II

IF YOU LIKED THIS...
Visit the Monument, a free-standing column, erected near the spot where the Great Fire began as a memorial. It is open for visitors to climb to the top for views of London.

PLAGUE AND FIRE

The Great Plague of 1665 and the Great Fire of 1666 were terrible disasters during Charles II's reign. London lost approximately 15% of its population to the plague, although the exact numbers are unknown. The Great Fire burned for four days, destroying most of the old City of London. Charles II and his brother, James, helped by pulling down buildings to create fire breaks.

RELIGION AND TITUS OATES

England was strongly Protestant in the 1600s. In 1678, a rogue called Titus Oates claimed to have discovered a Catholic plot to kill Charles II. Although Charles realised Oates was a liar, hysteria hit the nation and several innocent Catholics were executed.

'He never said a foolish thing nor ever did a wise one.'
Lord Rochester describing Charles II

'That's very true for my words are my own; my actions are my minister.'
Charles II in reply

JAMES II

BORN: October 1633 | **DIED:** 16 September 1701
REIGNED: 1685–8 | **MARRIED:** Anne Hyde (1660); Mary of Modena (1673)
CHILDREN (by Anne): Mary, Anne; (by Mary): James, Louisa

James II was a passionate Catholic in an equally passionate Protestant country. His refusal to give up his religion made him unpopular and resulted in him losing the throne after only three years as king.

MONMOUTH REBELLION

On Charles II's death without a legitimate heir, the throne went to his younger brother, James. Unpopular because of his Catholicism, James II faced a rebellion from Charles II's eldest illegitimate son, the Protestant Duke of Monmouth. Monmouth was defeated in 1685 and he and his followers were executed.

WEIRD AND WONDERFUL

It took five blows of the axe to behead the Duke of Monmouth; the executioner, Jack Ketch, was known for his clumsiness.

DECLARATION OF INDULGENCE, 1687

The Declaration of Indulgence guaranteed freedom of religion to everyone, regardless of whether they were Protestant or Catholic. Although James II was a Catholic and wanted everyone else to be, he had no desire to start a religious persecution against the Protestants.

'WARMING-PAN BABY'

When James II became king, his immediate heir was his daughter, Mary. As she was Protestant, it was decided

James II's strong Catholic beliefs lost him the throne

to tolerate James II until his death. However, the birth of a son to James in 1688 was regarded as a catastrophe, as that son, the future king, would undoubtedly be raised as a Catholic. Rumours spread saying that the child wasn't the king's baby; that he had been smuggled into the bedchamber in a warming pan. James II and his family fled to France for their own safety, as even the army had turned against him.

James II's son and grandson later led attempts to regain the throne (see p.76) but it was his daughter Mary II who succeeded to the throne in 1689.

WILLIAM III & MARY II

MARY: BORN: 30 April 1662 | **DIED:** 28 December 1694 | **REIGNED:** 1689–94
MARRIED: William of Orange | **CHILDREN:** died childless
WILLIAM: BORN: November 1650 | **DIED:** 8 March 1702 | **REIGNED:** 1689–1702
MARRIED: Mary, James II's daughter | **CHILDREN:** died childless

William III and Mary II were first cousins as well as husband and wife; both were grandchildren of Charles I. They became joint monarchs and saw the final defeat of James II in Ireland.

JOINT RULERS

Following James II's flight to France (see p.71), Parliament offered the crown to Mary. Although Mary was James II's daughter, she refused to accept the crown as sole ruler, taking it only on condition that her husband William was also voted king.

Parliament demanded certain conditions in return for giving William and Mary the crown. One such demand was to give Parliament the right to put through laws and taxes. As a result of these conditions, the role of the monarch became more constitutional than autocratic.

DID YOU KNOW?

James II's flight and the succession of William and Mary was called the 'Glorious Revolution', as no blood was shed.

BATTLE OF THE BOYNE

Two years after fleeing, James II returned to try and get support in Catholic Ireland. William's army of 36,000 men outnumbered James's army of 25,000, and James II lost the battle. He retreated to France, never to return to the British Isles again.

DEATH OF WILLIAM III

Mary II died in 1694 but William III outlived her by eight years. In 1702 William fell from his horse when it tripped over a mole hill. He developed a fever and died shortly afterwards. All over the country, the Jacobites, supporters of James II, raised their glasses in a toast to the 'little gentleman in black velvet', the mole who had caused this accident.

William III and Mary II were joint rulers

IF YOU LIKED THIS...

Visit Kensington Palace and Hampton Court Palace, both royal residences of William and Mary.

ANNE

 BORN: 6 February 1665 | **DIED:** 1 August 1714 | **REIGNED:** 1702–14
MARRIED: George of Denmark | **CHILDREN:** William, Duke of Gloucester

In Anne's reign, England and Scotland were united, and England won military victories under the Duke of Marlborough. Yet Anne's personal life was a tragic one, as she had to endure the deaths of all of her children.

ACT OF UNION

Although the crowns of England and Scotland had been united since 1603 (see p.66), the two countries still had separate Parliaments. In 1707 the Scottish Parliament had decided to vote for its own monarch after Anne's death, as she was childless, thus potentially splitting the crowns of England and Scotland after a century of unity. To ensure the continuation of England and Scotland under one monarch, England persuaded Scotland to agree to the Act of Union, through promises of increased trade under one Parliament.

Statue of Queen Anne

 IF YOU LIKED THIS...
Visit Blenheim Palace, near Oxford; still owned by the Dukes of Marlborough, and the birthplace of Winston Churchill, cousin of the ninth Duke of Marlborough.

BLENHEIM

In the early 1700s, England was at war with France over the question of the succession to the throne of Spain. The Battle of Blenheim in 1704 was the most outstanding success of this war, with the British army under the command of the Duke of Marlborough, the husband of Anne's best friend. As a reward, Anne gave him the money to build Blenheim Palace.

PERSONAL LIFE

Anne had the terrible experience of outliving all her children; out of her 18 pregnancies, only one child, the Duke of Gloucester, lived beyond infancy; but he later died at the age of 11.

 WEIRD AND WONDERFUL
Anne was so swollen and overweight when she died that she had to be buried in a square-shaped coffin.

The House of Hanover

By 1701, Mary II had died with no heir and the next in line, Anne, Mary II's sister, had no living children. This meant that the heir to the throne after Anne's death was her second cousin, George, Elector of Hanover. George was the next eligible monarch because the Act of Succession stated that only a Protestant could inherit the throne. The House of Hanover ruled throughout a period when the monarchy became completely constitutional, ruling through Parliament. It was also the period when the amount of territory Britain controlled abroad increased dramatically through the expansion of the British Empire.

The American War of Independence occurred during the Hanoverian reign

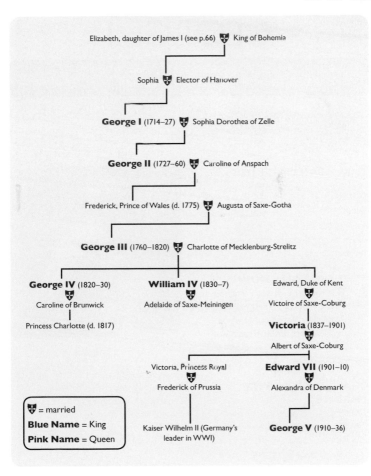

Elizabeth, daughter of James I (see p.66) 🛡 King of Bohemia

Sophia 🛡 Elector of Hanover

George I (1714–27) 🛡 Sophia Dorothea of Zelle

George II (1727–60) 🛡 Caroline of Anspach

Frederick, Prince of Wales (d. 1775) 🛡 Augusta of Saxe-Gotha

George III (1760–1820) 🛡 Charlotte of Mecklenburg-Strelitz

George IV (1820–30) 🛡 Caroline of Brunwick

Princess Charlotte (d. 1817)

William IV (1830–7) 🛡 Adelaide of Saxe-Meiningen

Edward, Duke of Kent 🛡 Victoire of Saxe-Coburg

Victoria (1837–1901) 🛡 Albert of Saxe-Coburg

Victoria, Princess Royal 🛡 Frederick of Prussia

Edward VII (1901–10) 🛡 Alexandra of Denmark

Kaiser Wilhelm II (Germany's leader in WWI)

George V (1910–36)

🛡 = married
Blue Name = King
Pink Name = Queen

GEORGE I

 BORN: May/June 1660 | **DIED:** June 1727 | **REIGNED:** 1714–27
MARRIED: Sophia Dorothea of Zelle | **CHILDREN:** George, Sophia Dorothea

George I was unpopular as he had no desire to be king and had locked his wife away for having a love affair. The United Kingdom had its first prime minister during his reign.

THE UNWILLING KING

George I stayed out of politics, leaving the business of the realm to the government. This and his lack of English led to Sir Robert Walpole, one of the leading ministers, becoming the first prime minister.

 DID YOU KNOW?
Although Sir Robert Walpole is known as the first prime minister, his official title was 'First Lord of the Treasury', a title which prime ministers still hold today.

CHALLENGE TO THE THRONE

James Stuart, the 'warming-pan baby' (see p.71), son of the deposed James II, led an army into Scotland in 1715 to try and regain the throne. This attempt failed, but a more serious one was to be made by his son 30 years later (see p.77).

FAMILY RELATIONS

George I had two mistresses, one called 'the elephant' because of her weight; and the other called 'the maypole' because of her height and thinness. Although he was very fond of them, there was constant tension between George and his family.

George I was a reluctant king

He imprisoned his wife, Sophia Dorothea, for taking a lover: she was locked up for 32 years until her death in 1726. He also detested his son, George II, leading to George and his wife setting up a rival court.

 WEIRD AND WONDERFUL
'The maypole' was so upset by George I's death that when a black raven flew into her apartment one day, she was convinced it was George, who had promised he would return to her; she took care of the raven until her death.

GEORGE II

BORN: October/November 1683 | **DIED:** 25 October 1760
REIGNED: 1727–60 | **MARRIED:** Caroline of Anspach
CHILDREN: Frederick, Anne, Amelia, Caroline, William, Mary, Louisa

George II's reign saw the defeat of Bonnie Prince Charlie at the Battle of Culloden and the expansion of British territories overseas. He ruled through clever politicians but was controlled by his wife until her death.

BONNIE PRINCE CHARLIE

In 1745, Bonnie Prince Charlie, grandson of the deposed King James II (see p.71), led an unsuccessful attempt to regain the crown. Gaining support in Scotland, he made his way through England, but turned back on reaching Derby, because of the lack of support from the English. At Culloden, in northern Scotland, his army was brutally defeated. Although he escaped, supporters of his cause were massacred on the orders of George II's son, William, Duke of Cumberland, leader of the English army.

After the deaths of Bonnie Prince Charlie and his brother without legitimate heirs, the line of James II died out.

IF YOU LIKED THIS...
Make a trip to the visitor centre at the site of the battle of Culloden.

EXPANSION OVERSEAS

In the 1750s, Robert Clive defeated the French armies in India, thus helping secure British control over India. At the same time, General Wolfe won a victory over the French in Canada at the Battle of Quebec. Both of these victories contributed to the creation of the British Empire (see p.84).

A CONTROLLING QUEEN

Queen Caroline ruled her husband so cleverly with the help of Sir Robert Walpole, that George was never aware of it.

DID YOU KNOW?
George II was the last British king to fight in battle, at Dettingen, against the French, in 1743.

George II in battle at Dettingen

GEORGE III

BORN: May/June 1738 | **DIED:** 29 January 1820 | **REIGNED:** 1760–1820
MARRIED: Charlotte of Mecklenburg-Strelitz
CHILDREN: George, Frederick, William, Charlotte, Edward, Augusta, Elizabeth, Ernest, Augustus, Adolphus, Mary, Sophia, Octavius, Alfred, Amelia

Crowned king at the age of 22, George III was a conscientious, fair monarch, but became famous for his outbreaks of porphyria (diagnosed as madness) and for the loss of the American colonies in his reign.

AMERICAN WAR OF INDEPENDENCE

By the 1770s, the 13 American colonies under British control, including Pennsylvania, Virginia and Maryland, were suffering under high taxation from Britain. Revolution broke out in 1775 and a year later, the Americans drew up the Declaration of Independence, based on the Magna Carta (see p.34), asserting their rights against the monarch, and declaring their determination to dissolve the connection between themselves and the United Kingdom. After defeat at Yorktown in 1781 the British army were forced to surrender. This loss was to haunt George III, even though, as a constitutional monarch, it was his ministers, not himself, who played the greatest part in this defeat.

A MAD KING?

In 1788, George III had his first attack of porphyria, a chemical imbalance which is often hereditary. In the late 18th century, this was diagnosed as madness. This went on for four months before he recovered.

However, he had another much more serious attack in 1811, brought on by the death of his youngest daughter, Amelia. He talked incessantly and often wildly, and became blind and deaf, making him completely unfit to rule. For the rest of his life, he lived in Windsor Castle, while his son George ruled during the period known as the Regency (see p.79).

IF YOU LIKED THIS...
Watch the film, *The Madness of King George*, about George III's attack of porphyria in 1788–9.

George III was ultimately a tragic king

THE REGENCY PERIOD

A regent rules for the monarch when the monarch is considered to be unfit to rule; this often happens when the monarch is a child, for example Henry VI's uncle acted as regent (see p.48). The most famous Regency period is that of George IV from 1811 to 1820.

GEORGE IV, THE PRINCE REGENT

Following a strict, rather stark childhood, the future George IV was extremely extravagant throughout his adult life, influencing the high-spending of this period. The lifestyle of the rich during the Regency was in stark contrast to the poverty caused by high unemployment and the Industrial Revolution.

WEIRD AND WONDERFUL

Two members of a gentlemen's club once bet £3,000 on which one of two raindrops would reach the bottom of the window first.

LIFE OF LEISURE

Gambling was one of the addictions of the rich and people would bet huge amounts of money on just about anything, often losing fortunes in one night.

LIFE OF POVERTY

At this time factory owners were starting to use steam-driven machinery to do the work, resulting in manual labourers losing their jobs. A group of protesters, the Luddites, broke into factories and smashed the machinery to try and keep their employment.

One of the consequences of this was the Peterloo Massacre in 1819, when a reform meeting against poverty was held and violently broken up by soldiers. Eleven people were killed and over 400 wounded.

The poverty and desperation of the poor during this period resulted in the Prince Regent becoming a hated figure due to his high spending and extravagant habits.

The Royal Pavilion in Brighton

GEORGE IV

BORN: 12 August 1762 | **DIED:** 26 June 1830 | **REIGNED:** 1820–30
MARRIED: Caroline of Brunswick | **CHILDREN:** Charlotte

George IV, previously the Prince Regent until the death of his father, was famous for his extravagance, his love of architecture and his mistresses, as well as the bad relationship he had with his wife.

GEORGE IV AND THE LADIES

George IV had several mistresses and even married a lady called Maria Fitzherbert in 1785. This marriage was illegal following the Royal Marriages Act of 1772 which stated that no member of the royal family under 25 could marry without the monarch's consent. In 1795 George married Caroline of Brunswick, but the marriage was a disaster and they only had one child before separating.

 WEIRD AND WONDERFUL

Allegedly, Caroline of Brunswick washed very rarely and when George IV met her for the first time, he demanded some brandy immediately and ran away to the other end of the room!

ARCHITECTURE

George IV had a love of architecture, and hired the architect John Nash to carry out a programme of building in London, including Regent Street and Carlton House Terrace. The most famous building

Portrait of George IV

he ordered was the Royal Pavilion in Brighton, built in an oriental style, with domes and minarets (see p.79). He asked for the original palace in the 1780s, but in 1815 gave orders to greatly expand it. The exterior alone cost in the region of £150,000 (over £6 million today).

 IF YOU LIKED THIS...
Visit the Royal Pavilion in Brighton as it has changed very little since the reign of George IV.

WELLINGTON AND WATERLOO

Throughout the first 15 years of the 19th century, Napoleon Bonaparte, Emperor of France, was gaining territory throughout Europe. Britain was under threat, but never conquered.

Two famous victories against Napoleon were the Battle of Trafalgar, where the Admiral of the Navy, Lord Nelson, was killed; and the Battle of Waterloo in 1815, Napoleon's final defeat when he was faced with the united Anglo-Dutch and the Prussian armies, commanded by the Duke of Wellington and Marshal Blucher. Napoleon was exiled to the island of St Helena after his defeat.

WILLIAM IV

BORN: 21 August 1765 | **DIED:** 20 June 1837 | **REIGNED:** 1830–7
MARRIED: Adelaide of Saxe-Meiningen
CHILDREN: died with no legitimate children

William IV was the third son of George III and only became king after his two elder brothers died without any surviving heirs. His short reign saw the Reform Act of 1832.

REFORM ACT

By 1830 there was a major problem in the voting system for Parliament. Voting constituencies had been drawn up years earlier and no longer reflected the make-up of the population. On the one hand, 'rotten boroughs', such as Old Sarum in Wiltshire, with a population of only 15 people, had as many as two members of Parliament to represent them, whereas fast-growing industrial towns such as Manchester had none. The opposition of the Tory party to the Reform Act, headed by the Duke of Wellington, caused rioting across the country until it was put through in 1832, effectively removing the rotten boroughs and ensuring that new towns were represented.

William IV had no legitimate heirs

DID YOU KNOW?
The Duke of Wellington was called the 'Iron Duke' because during the riots, he put iron shutters up on the windows of his London residence, Apsley House.

HEIR TO THE THRONE

Although William IV had 10 illegitimate children through his affair with an actress, Dorothy Jordan, he had no legitimate children with his wife, Adelaide. The heir to the throne, therefore, was his niece, the future Queen Victoria. When William became king, Victoria was only 11 years old. William IV absolutely hated Victoria's mother, due to her arrogance as the mother of the heir to the throne; at a state banquet, he started shouting at her as she had taken several rooms at Kensington Palace without his permission, saying that he had been 'grossly and continually insulted' by her. He was determined to live until Victoria was 18 and able to rule for herself without her mother acting as Regent. In this, he succeeded, dying one month after Victoria's 18th birthday.

VICTORIA

BORN: 24 May 1819 | **DIED:** 22 January 1901 | **REIGNED:** 1837–1901
MARRIED: Albert of Saxe-Coburg-Gotha | **CHILDREN:** Vicky, Bertie
(Edward VII), Alice, Alfred, Helena, Louise, Arthur, Leopold, Beatrice

Victoria ruled for 64 years, presiding over the height of the British
Empire (see p.84). She had an extremely happy marriage until the early
death of her husband and spent the rest of her life in mourning.

CHILDHOOD

Victoria's father died when she was a baby and she was brought up by her mother (see p.81). Her childhood was a rather unhappy one, during which she had very little contact with other children and saw her mother falling increasingly under the influence of her chief attendant Sir John Conroy. When Victoria became ill with typhoid fever at the age of 16, Conroy tried to make her sign a statement making him her private secretary upon becoming queen. She refused, even though she was so ill.

Victoria in her black mourning dress

IF YOU LIKED THIS...

Watch *The Young Victoria*, a film about Victoria's childhood and the early years of her reign. You can also visit Kensington Palace, where she was brought up.

PRINCE ALBERT

Two years after Victoria became monarch, she met her cousin, Prince Albert, whom she hadn't seen for three years. She fell immediately in love with him, and they were married in 1840. They had nine children, and Prince Albert organised the Great Exhibition of 1851, showing the latest inventions in science and industry.

Prince Albert died of typhoid fever at the age of only 42, leaving Victoria a widow for 40 years. For the rest of her life, she wore black in mourning.

DID YOU KNOW?

In 1839 Victoria took the unusual step of proposing to Prince Albert; as he was of much lower rank than her, she thought he would be too nervous to ask.

INDUSTRIAL REVOLUTION

The substitution of machinery for labourers had already caused nationwide unemployment and poverty (see p.79). People were forced to move to the towns to find employment, which caused overcrowded housing and bad sanitation, making the Victorian era one of awful poverty.

The extremes of wealth and poverty were written about by the famous novelist, Charles Dickens, in books such as *Oliver Twist* and *Hard Times*.

PRIME MINISTERS IN VICTORIA'S REIGN

Victoria had very strong opinions about people, particularly so in the case of several of her prime ministers. Her first prime minister was Lord Melbourne, with whom she developed a close relationship before her marriage, looking on him as a tutor in her early years as queen. Thirty years later, intense rivalry developed between the leaders of opposing political parties: Benjamin Disraeli and William Gladstone. Victoria got on very well with Disraeli and didn't like Gladstone at all, so she was never regarded as being a neutral figurehead in politics!

The Albert Memorial in Kensington Gardens

Kensington Palace where Victoria grew up

WEIRD AND WONDERFUL

When Victoria requested to visit Disraeli on his deathbed, he said, 'No, it is better not. She will only ask me to take a message to Albert!'

END OF HER REIGN

By the end of her reign, Victoria had become a symbol of continuity and stability. Her Golden Jubilee in 1887 and her Diamond Jubilee in 1897 caused huge celebrations. Her death at the age of 81 after a 64-year reign marked the passing of an era. One of her legacies is the vast British Empire she ruled over (see p.84). She is so far the longest-reigning monarch, although Elizabeth II may soon overtake her!

IF YOU LIKED THIS...

Visit the Albert Memorial in Kensington Gardens, on the site of the Great Exhibition and the South Kensington museums, built as a result of the money made from the Great Exhibition.

THE BRITISH EMPIRE

ORIGINS

The British Empire began in the reign of Elizabeth I, when explorers such as Sir Walter Raleigh were sailing the world and discovering new lands. They first concentrated on America, leading to the state of Virginia and then Massachusetts becoming colonies of Britain. Later, trading interests grew up in India, under the jurisdiction of the East India trading company. The empire was a commercial one, with Britain making sure that these countries traded with no-one else.

The loss of the American colonies as a result of the War of Independence in 1781 (see p.78) was a disaster, but Britain made up for it by gaining territories previously under French control, such as Trinidad and Tobago. Captain James Cook's explorations also led to New South Wales in Australia coming under Britain's control.

VICTORIA'S EMPIRE

During Victoria's reign, Britain expanded its territories to areas of Africa. Territories were often gained by force, as with Egypt and the Sudan, when armies were sent in. By the end of her reign, Victoria ruled over a quarter of the world's land area and a fifth of its population.

Territories in the British Empire included Canada, Australia, New Zealand, countries in Africa and Asia and several Caribbean islands, stretching so far around the globe that it was said the sun never set on it. This was the zenith of the British Empire with Britain becoming the most powerful nation in the world.

 DID YOU KNOW?
The British Empire, at its height, was the largest empire ever known.

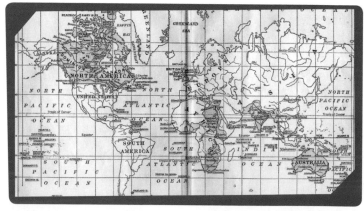

A map of the British empire in 1914

EDWARD VII

BORN: 9 November 1841 | **DIED:** 6 May 1910 | **REIGNED:** 1901–10
MARRIED: Alexandra of Denmark
CHILDREN: Albert Victor, George, Louisa, Victoria, Maud

Edward VII was the only monarch of the House of Saxe-Coburg-Gotha. His reign saw the peak of the suffragette movement and the formation of political alliances with France and Russia.

PRINCE OF WALES

Edward VII was a real ladies' man and amongst his most famous mistresses were Lillie Langtry, the Countess of Warwick and Alice Keppel. As Prince of Wales, he had already been involved in two scandals: one was as a witness in a court case when a guest at a house party he attended was accused of cheating at cards. He had also previously been involved in a divorce case, with the husband threatening to name him as one of his wife's lovers. Becoming king at the age of 59, he developed into a shrewd, able monarch

Edward VII was a wise monarch when he finally became king

DID YOU KNOW?
The wife of Prince Charles, Camilla Parker Bowles, is Alice Keppel's great-granddaughter.

SUFFRAGETTES

The call of 'Votes for Women!' carried on throughout the reign of Edward VII. The Suffragettes were desperate to get women the vote in general elections, as at that time, only men were allowed to vote. They would create disturbances by chaining themselves to the railings of 10 Downing Street and smashing windows, amongst other things. Women eventually got the vote in 1918.

FOREIGN POLICY

In 1904, Britain formed alliances with France and Russia. As Germany was regarded as being potentially aggressive under the leadership of Kaiser Wilhelm II, Edward VII's nephew, it was thought advisable to gain some allies. However the *Entente Cordiale* became one of the causes of the First World War (see p.88).

WEIRD AND WONDERFUL
Edward waited a long time to become King, serving as Prince of Wales for just over 59 years.

The Windsors

The House of Saxe-Coburg-Gotha was the royal family's name under Edward VII but when the First World War broke out George V thought that the name sounded too Germanic and so in 1917 he changed the name of the royal family to Windsor. The House of Windsor has ruled through a dramatic period of change in Britain, throughout two world wars and the decline of the British Empire overseas.

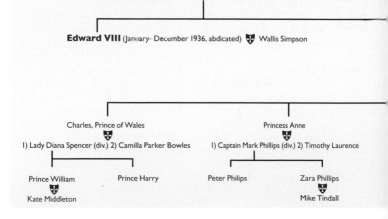

George V (1910–36) 🛡 Mary of Teck

Edward VIII (January–December 1936, abdicated) 🛡 Wallis Simpson

Charles, Prince of Wales 🛡
1) Lady Diana Spencer (div.) 2) Camilla Parker Bowles

Princess Anne 🛡
1) Captain Mark Phillips (div.) 2) Timothy Laurence

Prince William 🛡 Kate Middleton

Prince Harry

Peter Philips

Zara Phillips 🛡 Mike Tindall

Windsor Castle seen from the Great Park

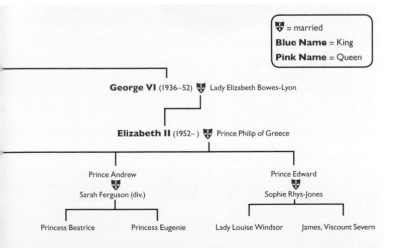

= married

Blue Name = King

Pink Name = Queen

George VI (1936–52) Lady Elizabeth Bowes-Lyon

Elizabeth II (1952–) Prince Philip of Greece

Prince Andrew
Sarah Ferguson (div.)

Prince Edward
Sophie Rhys-Jones

Princess Beatrice   Princess Eugenie

Lady Louise Windsor   James, Viscount Severn

GEORGE V

> **BORN:** 3 June 1865 | **DIED:** 20 January 1936 | **REIGNED:** 1910–36
> **MARRIED:** Mary of Teck | **CHILDREN:** David (future Edward VIII), Bertie (future George VI), Mary, Henry, George, John

George V carried out his role as king with firmness and stability, steering Britain through the horrors of the First World War and crisis in Ireland over the question of Home Rule.

BECOMING KING

As Edward VII's second son, George V didn't expect to sit on the throne at all and entered the Navy instead, which later earned him the nickname of 'Sailor King'. He became heir to the throne after the death of his elder brother, the Duke of Clarence, and married the Duke of Clarence's fiancée, Mary of Teck.

A 1917 George V penny

DID YOU KNOW?

George V was the first king to go on the radio, in a broadcast in 1932.

FIRST WORLD WAR

By 1914, European powers had formed alliances with other countries which pulled them into war. Britain, France and Russia (see p.85) allied against Germany, Austria-Hungary and Italy. Britain's main aim was to stop Germany dominating Europe and threatening the British Empire.

One of the worst battles of the war was the Somme in 1916, with a combined total of over one million soldiers on both sides killed. In spite of the high casualties, the battle was inconclusive. However, by mid-1918, the German army, forced back and suffering heavy losses, sued for peace.

IRISH HOME RULE

In Ireland, Catholics wanted independence from the United Kingdom but the Protestants were on the opposing side. The Easter Rising in Dublin in 1916 emphasised Ireland's desire to rule independently.

The rioters were defeated and executed, and the Protestants put up even fiercer resistance against independence. In 1921, this resulted in Ireland being divided in two, with Northern Ireland remaining a part of the UK.

 IF YOU LIKED THIS...
Visit St George's Chapel in Windsor where George V and his wife Mary are buried.

EDWARD VIII

 BORN: 23 June 1894 | **DIED:** 28 May 1972
REIGNED: January–December 1936 | **MARRIED:** Wallis Simpson
CHILDREN: died childless

Edward VIII was king for only 11 months before abdicating to marry Wallis Simpson. They lived the rest of their lives in France, Spain and the Bahamas.

ABDICATION CRISIS

Edward VIII was always a ladies' man and it was his mistress, Lady Furnell, who introduced him to the American Wallis Simpson, whom he became infatuated with. Stanley Baldwin, the prime minister, warned him that marriage to Wallis Simpson would be impossible for the King, as she had already been divorced twice. Edward, however, was adamant and abdicated, leaving his younger brother, George VI, to take over.

Edward VIII with Wallis Simpson

THE YEARS AFTER

After his abdication Edward VIII was given the title Duke of Windsor and married Wallis Simpson in 1937. They went to live in France but during the Second World War, they were sent to the Bahamas, part of the British Empire, where Edward was governor, later returning to France after the war.

The relations between Edward VIII and the rest of his family were always strained after the abdication, but on his death in 1972, he was buried in the royal

mausoleum at Frogmore near Windsor Castle, the burial place of Queen Victoria and Prince Albert. His wife was later buried next to him.

 DID YOU KNOW?
During the First World War Edward VIII served with the Grenadier Guards although he was not allowed to go to the front line.

'I have found it impossible. . . to discharge my duties as king. . . without the help and support of the woman I love.'
Edward VIII, on abdicating

GEORGE VI

BORN: 14 December 1895 | **DIED:** 6 February 1952
REIGNED: 1936–52 | **MARRIED:** Lady Elizabeth Bowes-Lyon
CHILDREN: Elizabeth, Margaret Rose

George VI reluctantly became king after the abdication of his brother, Edward VIII (see p.89). In spite of this, he reigned with determination and bravery, especially throughout the Second World War.

MARRIAGE TO LADY ELIZABETH BOWES-LYON

During his young adulthood, George VI was shy and self-conscious, but then met and fell in love with Lady Elizabeth Bowes-Lyon. When he proposed to her, she turned him down, unwilling to live her life in the public spotlight, but when he proposed a second time, she accepted. They had two daughters and lived a happy family life until the abdication of Edward VIII (see p.89).

THE ABDICATION

Edward VIII's abdication came as a blow to George VI, who was very reserved and

George VI's coronation

felt completely unprepared to become king. Suddenly thrust into the limelight, he proved to be an immensely capable monarch, ruling successfully throughout the horrors of the Second World War.

SPEECH IMPEDIMENT

George VI spoke with a stammer for years, possibly caused by being forced to write with his right hand throughout his childhood, although he was naturally left-handed. This made public speaking a nightmare for him. In 1926, he went to see the speech therapist Lionel Logue which proved to be an immense success. Logue taught him to speak slowly and carefully, with breathing exercises. The result was such that in a public speech in 1927, he was able to speak with only slight hesitations. The relationship between George VI and Lionel Logue was immortalised in the 2010 film *The King's Speech*.

THE BATTLE OF BRITAIN AND THE BLITZ

In 1939, the Second World War broke out, with Britain declaring war on Germany after Germany's invasion of Poland. 1940 proved to be a horrendous year for Europe, with European countries

falling one by one to the Germans, under the command of Adolf Hitler, Germany's leader.

Throughout the summer of 1940, the Battle of Britain was in full flow. The German air force bombed Royal Air Force bases all over south-east England, breaking the links of communication. The situation was reprieved when RAF planes succeeded in bombing Berlin. Hitler ordered the German air force to attack London in retaliation, which gave the south-east time to recover.

The George Cross

'Never in the field of human conflict was so much owed by so many to so few.'
Winston Churchill describing the fighter pilots

WEIRD AND WONDERFUL
The life expectancy of a pilot during the Battle of Britain was just four weeks.

From September 1940 to May 1941, London was crippled under the constant bombing. During this time, George VI refused to leave London and went around bombed areas (as did the prime minister, Winston Churchill) keeping morale high. By spring 1941, Britain was still undefeated and Hitler had to give up, suffering his first defeat since the war began.

IF YOU LIKED THIS...
Visit the Churchill War Museum in the underground bunkers used by the Cabinet during bombing raids in the Second World War.

DEFEAT OF GERMANY
By 1943, Germany was under pressure, following defeats in Africa and Russia. From the west, the Allied armies of Britain and America were approaching Germany; from the east, the Russian armies were also closing in. The D-Day victory on 6 June 1944, when the Allied armies successfully landed in German-occupied France, marked the beginning of the end for Hitler. By May 1945, Berlin was surrounded by these armies and Hitler committed suicide in his bunker. Japan, Germany's ally, was defeated in the Far East in August 1945, bringing the war to an end.

AFTER THE WAR
The Second World War wasn't the only crisis in George VI's reign. After the war, trouble started developing throughout the British Empire (see p.84) and the loss of India and Pakistan in 1947 was a severe blow. Worn out after the war and worried by the empire problems, George VI died in 1952 due to lung cancer.

DID YOU KNOW?
In 1940 George VI created the George Cross and the George Medal, to be awarded in recognition of acts of bravery.

ELIZABETH II

BORN: 21 April 1926 | **REIGN:** 1952 to present
MARRIED: Prince Philip of Greece
CHILDREN: Charles, Anne, Andrew, Edward

The Queen became monarch at the age of only 25. Reigning through a period of immense social change, her hard work and devotion to duty have earned her admiration and respect.

CHILDHOOD

At first, there seemed little possibility that Elizabeth would become Queen. When she was born, her uncle, Edward VIII was due to inherit and it was also possible that her parents would give birth to a son. Neither of these things happened though, and at the age of 11, on the accession of her father, George VI (see p.90), Princess Elizabeth became heiress to the throne.

After the Second World War (see p.90), Princess Elizabeth married Prince Philip of Greece and subsequently had four children. She became queen on the death of her father in 1952.

Elizabeth II on her coronation day

DID YOU KNOW?

In the Channel Islands the Queen holds the title of Duke of Normandy and Lord of Mann on the Isle of Man. These titles remain unchanged even when a queen sits on the throne.

CORONATION

The Queen's coronation in Westminster Abbey was the first to be televised; as a result, the Abbey was closed down for six months before the coronation to make the necessary preparations. In post-war Britain, where food was still rationed, the coronation was a great boost. The Queen rode in state carriages through the streets of London, witnessed by an estimated three million people. The royal family appeared on the balcony of Buckingham Palace, waving at the crowds; there was a fly-past from the Royal Air Force and the day culminated in a firework display.

THE COMMONWEALTH AND EUROPEAN UNION

At the time of the Queen's accession, the British Empire was ending. India declared its independence in 1947 (see p.91) and throughout the 1950s and 1960s, other countries did the same,

> **'Throughout all my life and with all my heart I shall strive to be worthy of your trust.'**
> The Queen's promise made in a radio broadcast after her coronation in 1953

including ones in Africa, the Caribbean and the Pacific. The British Empire was replaced by the Commonwealth, a federation of equal-ranking states, most of which were formerly part of the empire. Regular meetings are held by representatives who discuss subjects of mutual interest. The Queen is the head of the Commonwealth, but not recognised by all Commonwealth countries as head of state in their own particular country.

FAMILY TROUBLES

Three out of the Queen's four children have divorced their first partners: Prince Charles, Princess Anne and Prince Andrew. The Queen famously called 1992 her *annus horribilis*, as that year saw the marriage break-ups of Prince Charles and Prince Andrew and the divorce of Princess Anne. That year, there was also a fire at Windsor Castle, which destroyed a section of the State Apartments.

 IF YOU LIKED THIS...
Watch *The Queen* (2006) which revolves around the Queen's reaction to the death of Princess Diana in 1997.

THE MONARCHY TODAY

Since this period the popularity of the royal family has greatly improved, due partly to Prince Charles' devotion to his two sons, Princes William and Harry. In 2011, crowds gathered to watch the royal wedding of Prince William (who is second in line to the throne after Charles) to Kate Middleton, at Westminster Abbey.

Trooping the Colour to mark the Queen's birthday

More than 24 million people tuned in to watch the wedding on television.

The Queen is now the second-longest reigning monarch in British history, celebrating her 60th anniversary in 2012. She is loved for her unwavering stability and for her continuation of the pageantry and history associated with the monarchy.

Prince William and Kate Middleton married in 2011

USEFUL SOURCES

WEBSITES

www.bbc.co.uk/history
www.britroyals.com
www.english-heritage.org.uk
www.nationaltrust.org.uk
www.royal.gov.uk
www.royalcollection.org.uk

BOOKS

Britain's Royal Families, Alison Weir (Vintage, 2008)

The Kings & Queens of Scotland, Richard Oram (The History Press, 2001)

The Oxford Book of Royal Anecdotes, Elizabeth Longford (OUP, 1991)

Oxford Dictionary of British History, John Cannon (OUP, 2009)

This Sceptred Isle 55BC–1901, Christopher Lee (Penguin, 1998)

FILMS AND TELEVISION

Cromwell (1970): film about Cromwell and Charles I, with Richard Harris

Elizabeth R (1971): BBC TV series about Elizabeth I with Glenda Jackson

Henry V (1989): film based on the Shakespearean play starring Kenneth Branagh

The King's Speech (2010): film about George VI, with Colin Firth

The Lion in Winter (1968): film about Henry II, with Peter O'Toole

The Madness of King George (1994): film about George III with Nigel Hawthorne

The Queen (2006): film about Elizabeth II with Helen Mirren

The Young Victoria (2009): film about Queen Victoria's youth, with Emily Blunt

Buckingham Palace

PICTURE CREDITS

Photographs are reproduced with the permission of the following:

Alamy, © Robert Harding Picture Library Ltd: p.48

Alamy, © Stephen Dorey: p.40

Claire Parfey/Flickr: p.8 top left

Corbis, © Hulton-Deutsch Collection: p.11 bottom right; p.90

Corbis, © National Archives/Handout/ Reuteurs: p.8 top right

Corbis, © Reuteurs: p.11 top right

© **Getty Images**: Front cover; p.89; p.93 bottom right

Getty, © Henri Gascard: p.71

Getty, © Hans the Younger Holbein: p.10 centre left; p.56

Heritage-Images, © The British Library: p.37; p.72

Heritage images, © The Print Collector: p.6 top right, bottom right; p.27, p.32 top; p.51; p.66

Heritage Images, © Stapleton Historical Collection: p.59 bottom left

istock: p.7 bottom right; p.8 centre right; p.9 centre right, bottom right; p.10 top left; p.11 top left; p.17; p.25; p.26; p.29; p.35 top

left; p.45; p.46; p.55 top left; p.58 bottom right; p.59 top right, centre left, bottom right; p.60; p.61; p.65; p.93 top right

Jim Linwood/Flickr: p.39

Mary Evans Picture Library:p./7

Mary Evans, © Illustrated London News Ltd: p.36

© **National Portrait Gallery**: p.32 bottom left

Shadowgate/Flickr: p.6 bottom left; p.12

Thinkstock: p.4; p.5; p.6 top left, centre right; p.7 top, centre right, centre left, bottom left; p.8 centre left, bottom left, bottom right; p.9 top left and right, centre left, bottom left; p.10 top right, centre right, bottom left and right; p.11 centre left and right, bottom left; p.13; p.15; p.16; p.18; p.19; p.20; p.21 top, bottom left; p.23; p.24; p.30 top left, bottom left; p.31; p.33; p.34; p.35 bottom right; p.38; p.40 bottom; p.41; p.44; p.47; p.49; p.50; p.53; p.54; p.55 bottom right; p.57 top left, bottom; p.58 top left, top right; p.62; p.63 top right, centre left; p.67; p.68; p.69; p.70; p.73; p.74; p.75; p.78; p.79; p.80; p.81; p.82; p.83 top right, bottom left; p.84; p.85; p.87; p.88; p.91; p.94

© **V&A Images**: p.92

GET 25% OFF
Royal London

Discover the people and places that make London's **royal heritage** the most renowned in the world. From **Henry VIII's** favourite view to **Will and Kate's** favourite shops *Royal London* reveals the scandal, mystery and romance of the capital's history.

Includes maps of all London's royal hotspots

ONLY £5.25
was £6.99 RRP

Royal
London

The Haunts and Hideouts of Kings and Queens from London's Past and Present

Visit **www.crimsonbooks.co.uk** to get **25% off.**

To claim your discount simply enter the code 'Heritage' at the checkout*

Terms and conditions available online.

crimson
www.crimsonbooks.co.uk